Workshop on Automatic Summarization for Different Genres, Media and Language 2011

Held at ACL HLT 2011

Portland, Oregon, USA
23 June 2011

ISBN: 978-1-61839-248-0

Printed from e-media with permission by:

Curran Associates, Inc.
57 Morehouse Lane
Red Hook, NY 12571

proceedings.com

Some format issues inherent in the e-media version may also appear in this print version.

Printed by Curran Associates, Inc. (2011)

Association for Computational Linguistics
209 N. Eighth Street
Stroudsburg, Pennsylvania 18360

Phone: 1-570-476-8006
Fax: 1-570-476-0860

acl@aclweb.org

Additional copies of this publication are available from:

Curran Associates, Inc.
57 Morehouse Lane
Red Hook, NY 12571 USA
Phone: 845-758-0400
Fax: 845-758-2634
Email: curran@proceedings.com
Web: www.proceedings.com

Introduction

Welcome to the ACL Workshop on Automatic Summarization for Different Genres, Media, and Languages!

Our motivation for organizing this workshop has been the need many researchers in the field have seen, to come together to discuss various new issues that the field is facing as more and more summarization work is being conducted for domains beyond newswire and broadcast news. Extractive summarization of newswire text has dominated summarization research for over a decade. Large corpora of machine- and human-authored summaries have been collected and evaluation has been standardized to a large extent. As work on different genres, media and languages, such as voice mail, email, meetings, broadcast conversations, lectures, chat, blogs and scientific articles becomes more prominent, the need to precisely define tasks, to provide corpora to support comparison between approaches, and to identify desirable evaluation metrics is becoming increasingly urgent. We hope that this workshop will provide a valuable opportunity for all participants to present their work and to engage in discussion about the issues and problems they face, and how we can best support the changing nature of the field.

We have an exciting mix of papers. Some introduce novel summarization tasks: abstractive summarization of line graphs from popular media, summarization of Wikipedia articles with increasing popularity, summarization of chat for the military. Others present new approaches to summarization tasks that have been gaining popularity in recent years, such as summarization of spoken meetings and scientific articles. We are fortunate to have a paper from the organizers of the Text Analysis Conferences (TAC). This paper presents an in-depth analysis of the newest task adopted for the evaluation that, while still based on news, promotes the use of abstractive approaches and makes it possible to track the types of information people consider important and summary-worthy. Finally, we have a reminder that continuity in research focus truly helps to understand a domain and sharpen our understanding of prior approaches to the task; we will hear about some significant improvements in the topic model approach that has proven to be so successful for multi-document summarization of news.

In addition to our diverse program, we will have two invited presentations that will give a more structured overview of the emerging research in summarization. Gabriel Murray's talk is titled "Trends in Abstracting Conversations" and Pascale Fung's is "Structural Summarization of Spoken Documents and its Application to Meeting Minute Generation".

We look forward to a stimulating and engaging workshop!

Ani Nenkova, Julia Hirschberg, and Yang Liu

Organizers:

Ani Nenkova, Univeristy of Pennsylvania
Julia Hirschberg, Columbia University
Yang Liu, University of Texas at Dallas

Program Committee:

Annie Louis (Univ. of Pennsylvania)
Benoit Favre (LIUM, France)
Bonnie Dorr (UMD)
Chin-Yew Lin (Microsoft Research, China)
Daniel Gillick (ICSI)
Dilek Hakkani-Tur (Microsoft)
Fei Liu (UT Dallas)
Gabriel Murray (UBC, Canada)
Gerald Penn (Univ. of Toronto, Canada)
Hakan Ceylan (Yahoo)
Izhak Shafran (Oregon Health and Science University)
Kathy McKeown (Columbia University)
Lucy Vanderwende (Microsoft Research)
Pascale Fung (HKUST, Hong Kong)
Ryan McDonald (Google)
Sameer Maskey (IBM)
Steve Renals (Edinburgh, UK)
Thomas Kleinbauer (DFKI, Germany)
Xiaojun Wan (Peking University, China)

Invited Speakers:

Pascale Fung (HKUST, Hong Kong)
Gabriel Murray (UBC, Canada)

Table of Contents

Workshop Program

09:15-09:30 Introduction

09:30-10:30 Invited talk: Pascale Fung
Structural Summarization of Spoken Documents and its Application to Meeting Minute Generation

10:30-11:00 Morning break

11:00-12:30 Poster session

12:30-14:30 Lunch break

14:30-15:30 Invited talk: Gabriel Murray
Trends in Abstracting Conversations

15:30-16:00 Afternoon break

16:00-17:30 Discussion

Posters

Plans Toward Automated Chat Summarization
David C. Uthus and David W. Aha

Towards Multi-Document Summarization of Scientific Articles:Making Interesting Comparisons with SciSumm
Nitin Agarwal, Ravi Shankar Reddy, Kiran Gvr and Carolyn Penstein Rosé

Summarizing Decisions in Spoken Meetings
Lu Wang and Claire Cardie

Who wrote What Where: Analyzing the content of human and automatic summaries
Karolina Owczarzak and Hoa Dang

WikiTopics: What is Popular on Wikipedia and Why
Byung Gyu Ahn, Benjamin Van Durme and Chris Callison-Burch

Abstractive Summarization of Line Graphs from Popular Media
Charles Greenbacker, Peng Wu, Sandra Carberry, Kathleen McCoy and Stephanie Elzer

Extractive Multi-Document Summaries Should Explicitly Not Contain Document Specific Content
Rebecca Mason and Eugene Charniak

Posters from other workshops and main conference

Text Specificity and Impact on Quality of News Summaries
Annie Louis and Ani Nenkova
Workshop on Monolingual Text-To-Text Generation at ACL-HLT 2011

A Pilot Study of Opinion Summarization in Conversationss
Dong Wang and Yang Liu
ACL-HLT 2011 main conference

Why is "SXSW" Trending? Exploring Multiple Text Sources for Twitter Topic Summarization
Fei Liu, Yang Liu, and Fuliang Weng
Workshop on Language in Social Media at ACL-HLT 2011

Plans Toward Automated Chat Summarization

David C. Uthus
NRC/NRL Postdoctoral Fellow
Washington, DC 20375
david.uthus.ctr@nrl.navy.mil

David W. Aha
Naval Research Laboratory (Code 5514)
Washington, DC 20375
david.aha@nrl.navy.mil

Abstract

We describe the beginning stages of our work on summarizing chat, which is motivated by our observations concerning the information overload of US Navy watchstanders. We describe the challenges of summarizing chat and focus on two chat-specific types of summarizations we are interested in: thread summaries and temporal summaries. We then discuss our plans for addressing these challenges and evaluation issues.

1 Introduction

We are investigating methods to summarize real-time chat room messages to address a problem in the United States military: information overload and the need for automated techniques to analyze chat messages (Budlong et al., 2009). Chat has become a popular mode of communications in the military (Duffy, 2008; Eovito, 2006). On US Navy ships, watchstanders (i.e., personnel who continuously monitor and respond to situation updates during a ship's operation, Stavridis and Girrier (2007)) are responsible for numerous duties including monitoring multiple chat rooms. When a watchstander reports to duty or returns from an interruption, they have to familiarize themselves with the current situation, including what is taking place in the chat rooms. This is difficult with the multiple chat rooms opened simultaneously and new messages continuously arriving. Similarly, Boiney et al. (2008) observed that with US Air Force operators, when they returned to duty from an interruption, another operator in the same room verbally updates them with a summary of what had recently taken place in the chat rooms and where they can find the important information. Both of these situations are motivations for chat summarization, since watchstanders and operators could use automatically generated summaries to quickly orient themselves with the current situation.

While our motivation is from a military perspective, chat summarization is also applicable to other domains. For example, chat is used for communication in multinational companies (Handel and Herbsleb, 2002), open source meetings (Shihab et al., 2009; Zhou and Hovy, 2005), and distance learning (Osman and Herring, 2007). Summarization could aid people who missed meetings or students who wish to study past material in a summarized format.

Even though chat summarization has many potential uses, there has been little research on this topic (Section 3). One possible reason for this is that chat is a difficult medium to analyze: its characteristics make it difficult to apply traditional NLP techniques. It has uncommon features such as frequent use of abbreviations, acronyms, deletion of subject pronouns, use of emoticons, abbreviation of nicknames, and stripping of vowels from words to reduce number of keystrokes (Werry, 1996). Chat is also characterized by conversation threads becoming entangled due to multiple conversations taking place simultaneously in *multiparticipant chat*, i.e., chat composed of three or more users within the same chat room (Herring, 1999; Herring, 2010). The interwoven threads then make it more difficult to comprehend individual conversations.

The rest of this paper describes our challenges

Proceedings of the Workshop on Automatic Summarization for Different Genres, Media, and Languages, pages 1–7,
Portland, Oregon, June 23, 2011.

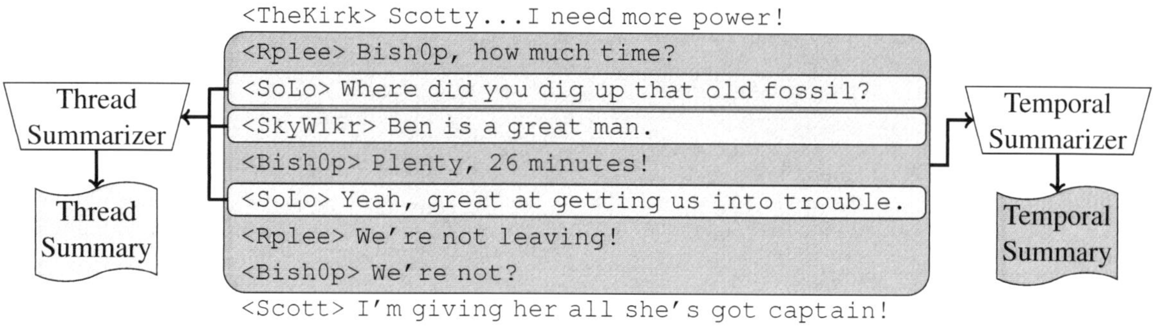

Figure 1: Process for generating thread and temporal summaries from a chat log.

in chat summarization. We define two chat-related types of summarizations we are investigating (Section 2) and describe related work (Section 3). Furthermore, we give an overview of our planned approach to these challenges (Section 4) and also address relevant evaluation issues (Section 5).

2 Our Summarization Challenge

Our research goal is to summarize chat in real-time. Summaries need to be updated with every new chat message that arrives, which can be difficult in high-tempo situations. For these summarizations, we seek an abstract, compact format, allowing watch-standers to quickly situate themselves with the current situation.

We are investigating two types of summarization: *thread summaries* and *temporal summaries*. These allow a user to actively decide how much summarization they need. This can be useful when a user needs a summary of a long, important conversation, or when they need a summary of what has taken place since they stopped monitoring a chat room.

2.1 Thread Summarization

The first type of summarization we are investigating is a thread summary. This level of summarization targets individual conversation threads. An example of this is shown in Figure 1, where a summary would be generated of the messages highlighted in green, which all belong to the same conversation. An example output summary may then be:

> SoLo and SkyWlkr are talking about Ben. SkyWlkr thinks he's great, SoLo thinks he causes trouble.

As shown, this will allow for a summarization to focus solely on messages within a conversation between users. A good summary for thread summarization will answer three questions: *who* is conversing, *what* they are conversing about, and what is the *result* of their conversation. With our example, the summary answers all three questions: it identifies the two speakers SoLo and SkyWlkr, it identifies that they are talking about Ben, and that the result is SkyWlkr thinks Ben is great while SoLo thinks Ben causes trouble.

The key challenge to thread summarization will be finding, extracting, and summarizing the individual conversation threads. This requires the ability to detect and extract threads, which has become of great interest in recent research (Duchon and Jackson, 2010; Elsner and Charniak, 2010; Elsner and Schudy, 2009; Ramachandran et al., 2010; Wang and Oard, 2009). Thread disentanglement and summarization will have to be done online, with conversation threads being updated every time a new message appears. Another challenge will be processing incomplete conversations, since some messages may be incorrectly classified into the wrong conversation threads. These issues will need to be addressed as this research progresses.

2.2 Temporal Summarization

The other form of summarization we seek is a temporal summary. We want to allow users to dynamically specify the temporal interval of summarization needed. In addition, a user will be able to specify the level of detail of the summary, which will be explained further later in this section. An example of a user selecting a temporal summary can be seen in

Figure 1. A summary will be generated of only the text that the user selected, which is shaded in blue. An example output summary may then be:

> Rplee and Bish0p disagree if there is enough time to stay. SoLo and SkyWlkr are talking about Ben.

A good summary for this task will answer the following question: what conversations have taken place within the specified temporal interval. In some cases depending on the user's preference, not all conversations will be included in the summary. When not all conversations are included, then a good summary will consist of the most important conversations and exclude those which are deemed less important. The amount of detail to be presented for each individual conversation will be determined by the temporal interval and the level of detail requested by the user, which is discussed later in this section.

The summaries will need to be generated after a user selects the temporal interval. To aid in this, we envision that the summarizer will leverage the thread summaries. Conversations threads, along with their abstracts, will be stored in memory, and these will be updated every time a new message is received. The temporal summarizer can then use the thread summaries to generate the temporal summaries.

A user will also be able to specify the level of detail in the summary in addition to the temporal interval. When generating a temporal summary, a higher level of detail will result in a longer summary, with the highest level of detail resulting in a summary consisting of all the thread summaries within the temporal interval. In the case of a lower level of detail, the summarizer will have to determine which threads are important to include, and further abstract them to create a smaller summary. The benefit of allowing the user to specify the level of detail is so that they can determine how much detail they need based on personal requirements. For example, if someone only has a short amount of time to read a summary, then they can specify a low level of detail to quickly understand the important points discussed within the temporal interval they want covered.

Temporal summaries present additional challenges to address. The primary one is determining which conversation threads to include in the summary, which require a ranking metric. Additionally, there is an issue of whether to include a conversation thread if all messages do not all fall within the temporal interval. For example, if there is a long conversation composed of many messages, and only one message falls within the temporal interval, should it then be included or discarded? These issues will also need to be addressed as this research progresses.

2.3 Chat Corpora

An additional challenge of this work is finding a suitable chat corpus that can be used for testing and evaluating summarization applications. Most chat corpora do not have any summaries associated with them to use for a gold standard, making evaluations difficult. This evaluation difficulty is described further in Section 5.

Currently, we are aware of two publicly available chat logs with associated summaries. One of these is the GNUe Traffic archive[1], which contains human-created summaries in the form of a newsletter based primarily on Internet Relay Chat (IRC) logs. Working with these chat logs requires abstractive (i.e., summaries consisting of system-generated text) and extractive (i.e., summaries consisting of text copied from source material) applications (Lin, 2009), as the summaries are composed of both human narration and quotes from the chat logs.

The other corpus is composed of chat logs and summaries of a group of users roleplaying a fantasy game over IRC.[2] The summaries are of an abstractive form. Creating summaries for these logs is more difficult since the summaries take on different styles. Some summarize the events of each character (e.g., their actions during a battle), while others are more elaborate in describing the chat events using a strong fantasy style.

3 Related Work

Summarization has been applied to many different media (Lin, 2009; Spärck Jones, 2007), but only Zhou and Hovy (2005) have worked on summarizing chat. They investigated summarizing chat logs in order to create summaries comparable to the human-made GNUe Traffic digests, which were described in Section 2.3. Their approach clustered partial mes-

[1] http://kt.earth.li/GNUe/index.html

[2] http://www.bluearch.net/night/history.html

sages under identified topics, then created a collection of summaries, with one summary for each topic. In their work, they were using an extractive form of summarization. For evaluation, they rewrote the GNUe Traffic digests to partition the summaries into summaries for each topic, making it easier to compare with their system-produced summaries. Their approach performed well, outperforming a baseline approach and achieving an F-score of 0.52.

There has also been work on summarization of media which share some similarities to chat. For example, Zechner (2002) examined summarization of multiparty dialogues and Murray et al. (2005) examined summarization of meeting recordings. Both of these media share in common with chat the difficulty of summarizing conversations with multiple participants. A difference with chat is that both of these publications focused on one conversation sequentially while chat is characterized by multiple, unrelated conversations taking place simultaneously. Newman and Blitzer (2003) described the beginning stages of their work on summarizing archived discussions of newsgroups and mailing lists. This has some similarity with conversations, but a difference is that newsgroups and mailing lists have metadata to help differentiate the threaded conversations. Additional differences between chat and these other media can be seen in the unusual features not found in other forms of written texts, as described earlier in Section 1.

4 Planned Approach

We envision taking a three step approach to achieve our goals for this research. We will abstract this to a non-military domain, so that it is more accessible to the research community.

4.1 Foundation

The first step is to focus on improving techniques for summarizing chat logs in general to create a foundation for future extensions. With the only approach so far having been by Zhou and Hovy (2005), it is unknown whether this is the best path for chat summarization, nor is it known how well it would work for real-time chat. Also, since its publication, new techniques for analyzing multiparticipant chat have been introduced, particularly in thread disentanglement, which could improve chat summarization.

We hypothesize that constructing an approach that incorporates new techniques and ideas, while addressing lessons learned by Zhou and Hovy (2005), can result in a more robust chat summarizer that can generate summaries online. A part of this process will include examining other techniques for summarization, drawing on ideas from related work discussed in Section 3, such as leveraging latent semantic analysis (Murray et al., 2005). Furthermore, we will incorporate past work on dialogue act tagging in chat (Wu et al., 2005) to both improve summarization and create a framework for the next two steps. However, there is one limitation with their work: the templates used for tagging were manually created, which is both time-intensive and fragile. To overcome this, we plan to use an unsupervised learning approach to discover dialogue acts (Ritter et al., 2010).

4.2 Thread Extension

The second step will be to extend summarization to thread summaries. This will require leveraging thread disentanglement techniques, with the possibility of using multiple techniques to improve the capability of finding whole conversation threads. For the summary generations, we will first create extractive summaries before extending the summarizer to generate abstractive summaries. In addition, we will address the problem of incomplete conversations for the cases when not all messages can be extracted correctly, or when not all the messages of a conversation are available due to joining a chat room in the middle of a conversation.

Another task will be the creation of a suitable corpus for this work. As discussed in Section 2.3, there are only two known corpora with associated summaries. Neither of these corpora are well suited for thread summarization since the summaries are not targeted towards answering specific questions (see Section 2.1), making evaluations difficult. We plan on creating a corpus by extending an existing thread disentanglement corpus (Elsner and Charniak, 2010). This corpus consists of technical chat on IRC related to Linux, and has been annotated by humans for conversation threads. We will expand this corpus to include both extractive and abstractive summaries for each of the threads. The advantage of using this corpus, beyond the annotations, is that it is topic-focused, which is a closer match of what one would expect to see in the military domain compared to social chat.

4.3 Temporal Extension

The third and final step will be to extend summarization to temporal summaries. The key point of this will be to extend the summarization capability so that a user can specify the level of detail within the summary, which will then determine the length of the summary and how much to include from the thread summaries. This will then involve creating a ranking metric for the different conversations. Unlike the thread extension, no additional abstraction will be needed. Instead, the temporal extension will reuse the thread summaries, and reduce their length by ranking the sentences within the individual summaries as done with traditional text summarization. Additionally, the problem of conversation threads containing messages both inside and outside the temporal interval will need to be addressed.

As with the thread extension, a corpora will need to be created for this work. We expect that this will build on the corpora used for the thread extension. This will then require additional summaries to be created for different levels of temporal intervals and detail. To make this task feasible, we will restrict the number of possible temporal intervals and levels of detail to only a few options.

5 Evaluation Issues

A major issue in summarization is evaluation (Spärck Jones, 2007), which is also a concern for this work. One problem for evaluation is the lack of suitable gold standards, as described in Section 2.3. Another problem is that we plan on working with abstractive forms in the future.

For the foundation step, we can follow the same procedures as Zhou and Hovy (2005), which would allow us to compare our results with theirs. This would restrict the work to only an extractive form for comparisons, though it is possible to extend to abstract comparisons due to the gold standards being composed of both extractive and abstractive means.

Evaluation for the thread and temporal extensions will require additional work due to both the lack of suitable gold standards and our need for abstractive summaries instead of extractive summaries. The evaluations will include both intrinsic (i.e., how well the summarizer is able to meet its objectives) and extrinsic evaluations (i.e., how well the summaries allow the user to perform their task, Spärck Jones (2007)). For the intrinsic evaluations, we will use both automated techniques (e.g., ROUGE[3]) and human assessors for evaluating both the thread and temporal summarizations. Some concerns for evaluation is that with the thread summaries, evaluation will be impacted by how accurately conversation threads can be extracted. With the temporal summaries, the temporal intervals and the level of detail determines the length and detail of the summary.

For the extrinsic evaluations, this research will be evaluated as part of a larger project, which will include human subject studies. Subjects will be situated in a simulated watchstander environment, must monitor three computer monitors simultaneously (one of which will contain live chat) while also listening to radio communications. Testing of our chat summarization methods will be done in collaboration with testing on 3D audio cueing to investigate and evaluate whether these technologies can help watchstanders combat information overload.

6 Conclusion

We have presented the challenges we face in chat summarization. Our goal for this research is that it will result in a robust chat summarizer which is able to generate abstract summaries in real-time. This is a difficult, exciting domain, with many possible applications. We have shown that the difficulties are due to the chat medium itself, lack of suitable data, and difficulties of evaluation.

Acknowledgements

Thanks to NRL for funding this research and to the reviewers for their valuable feedback. David Uthus performed this work while an NRC postdoctoral fellow located at the Naval Research Laboratory. The views and opinions contained in this paper are those of the authors and should not be interpreted as representing the official views or policies, either expressed or implied, of NRL or the DoD.

[3]http://berouge.com/default.aspx

References

Lindsley G. Boiney, Bradley Goodman, Robert Gaimari, Jeffrey Zarrella, Christopher Berube, and Janet Hitzeman. 2008. Taming multiple chat room collaboration: Real-time visual cues to social networks and emerging threads. In *Proceedings of the Fifth International ISCRAM Conference*, pages 660–668. ISCRAM.

Emily R. Budlong, Sharon M. Walter, and Ozgur Yilmazel. 2009. Recognizing connotative meaning in military chat communications. In *Proceedings of Evolutionary and Bio-Inspired Computation: Theory and Applications III*. SPIE.

Andrew Duchon and Cullen Jackson. 2010. Chat analysis for after action review. In *Proceedings of the Interservice/Industry Training, Simulation & Education Conference*. I/ITSEC.

LorRaine T. Duffy. 2008. DoD collaboration and chat systems: Current status and way ahead. In *Proceedings of the International Conference on Semantic Computing*, pages 573–576. IEEE Computer Society.

Micha Elsner and Eugene Charniak. 2010. Disentangling chat. *Computational Linguistics*, 36(3):389–409.

Micha Elsner and Warren Schudy. 2009. Bounding and comparing methods for correlation clustering beyond ILP. In *Proceedings of the Workshop on Integer Linear Programming for Natural Language Processing*, pages 19–27. ACL.

Bryan A. Eovito. 2006. The impact of synchronous text-based chat on military command and control. In *Proceedings of the Command and Control Research and Technology Symposium*. CCRP.

Mark Handel and James D. Herbsleb. 2002. What is chat doing in the workplace? In *Proceedings of the 2002 ACM Conference on Computer Supported Cooperative Work*, pages 1–10. ACM.

Susan C. Herring. 1999. Interactional coherence in CMC. In *Proceedings of the Thirty-Second Annual Hawaii International Conference on System Sciences*. IEEE Computer Society.

Susan C. Herring. 2010. Computer-mediated conversation: Introduction and overview. *Language@Internet*, 7. Article 2.

Jimmy Lin. 2009. Summarization. In M. Tamer Özsu and Ling Liu, editors, *Encyclopedia of Database Systems*. Springer.

Gabriel Murray, Steve Renals, Jean Carletta, and Johanna Moore. 2005. Evaluating automatic summaries of meeting recordings. In *Proceedings of the ACL Workshop on Intrinsic and Extrinsic Evaluation Measures for Machine Translation and/or Summarization*, pages 33–40. ACL.

Paula S. Newman and John C. Blitzer. 2003. Summarizing archived discussions: A beginning. In *Proceedings of the 8th International Conference on Intelligent User Interfaces*, pages 273–276. ACM.

Gihan Osman and Susan C. Herring. 2007. Interaction, facilitation, and deep learning in cross-cultural chat: A case study. *The Internet and Higher Education*, 10(2):125–141.

Sowmya Ramachandran, Randy Jensen, Oscar Bascara, Todd Denning, and Shaun Sucillon. 2010. Automated chat thread analysis: Untangling the web. In *Proceedings of the Interservice/Industry Training, Simulation & Education Conference*. I/ITSEC.

Alan Ritter, Colin Cherry, and Bill Dolan. 2010. Unsupervised modeling of Twitter conversations. In *Proceedings of Human Language Technologies: The 11th Annual Conference of the North American Chapter of the Association for Computational Linguistics*, pages 172–180. ACL.

Emad Shihab, Zhen Ming Jiang, and Ahmed E. Hassan. 2009. Studying the use of developer IRC meetings in open source projects. In *Proceedings of the IEEE International Conference on Software Maintenance*, pages 147–156. IEEE Computer Society.

Karen Spärck Jones. 2007. Automatic summarising: The state of the art. *Information Processing & Management*, 43(6):1449–1481.

James Stavridis and Robert Girrier. 2007. *Watch Officer's Guide: A Handbook for All Deck Watch Officers*. Naval Institute Press, fifteenth edition.

Lidan Wang and Douglas W. Oard. 2009. Context-based message expansion for disentanglement of interleaved text conversations. In *Proceedings of Human Language Technologies: The 2009 Annual Conference of the North American Chapter of the Association for Computational Linguistics*, pages 200–208. ACL.

Christopher C. Werry. 1996. Linguistic and interactional features of Internet Relay Chat. In Susan C. Herring, editor, *Computer-Mediated Communication: Linguistic, Social and Cross-Cultural Perspectives*, pages 47–64. John Benjamins.

Tianhao Wu, Faisal M. Khan, Todd A. Fisher, Lori A. Shuler, and William M. Pottenger. 2005. Posting act tagging using transformation-based learning. In Tsau Young Lin, Setsuo Ohsuga, Churn-Jung Liau, Xiaohua Hu, and Shusaku Tsumoto, editors, *Foundations of Data Mining and Knowledge Discovery*, volume 6 of *Studies in Computational Intelligence*, pages 321–331. Springer Berlin / Heidelberg.

Klaus Zechner. 2002. Automatic summarization of open-domain multiparty dialogues in diverse genres. *Computational Linguistics*, 28(4):447–485.

Liang Zhou and Eduard Hovy. 2005. Digesting virtual "geek" culture: The summarization of technical Internet Relay Chats. In *Proceedings of the 43rd Annual Meeting on Association for Computational Linguistics*, pages 298–305. ACL.

Towards Multi-Document Summarization of Scientific Articles:Making Interesting Comparisons with SciSumm

Nitin Agarwal
Language Technologies Institute
Carnegie Mellon University
nitina@cs.cmu.edu

Kiran Gvr
Language Technologies Resource Center
IIIT-Hyderabad, India
kiran_gvr@students.iiit.ac.in

Ravi Shankar Reddy
Language Technologies Resource Center
IIIT-Hyderabad, India
krs_reddy@students.iiit.ac.in

Carolyn Penstein Rosé
Language Technologies Institute
Carnegie Mellon University
cprose@cs.cmu.edu

Abstract

We present a novel unsupervised approach to the problem of multi-document summarization of scientific articles, in which the document collection is a list of papers cited together within the same source article, otherwise known as a co-citation. At the heart of the approach is a topic based clustering of fragments extracted from each co-cited article and relevance ranking using a query generated from the context surrounding the co-cited list of papers. This analysis enables the generation of an overview of common themes from the co-cited papers that relate to the context in which the co-citation was found. We present a system called SciSumm that embodies this approach and apply it to the 2008 ACL Anthology. We evaluate this summarization system for relevant content selection using gold standard summaries prepared on principle based guidelines. Evaluation with gold standard summaries demonstrates that our system performs better in content selection than an existing summarization system (MEAD). We present a detailed summary of our findings and discuss possible directions for future research.

1 Introduction

In this paper we present a novel, unsupervised approach to multi-document summarization of scientific articles. While the field of multi-document summarization has achieved impressive results with collections of news articles, summarization of collections of scientific articles is a strikingly different problem. Multi-document summarization of news articles amounts to synthesizing details about the same story as it has unfolded over a variety of reports, some of which contain redundant information. In contrast, each scientific article tells its own research story. Even with papers that address similar research questions, the argument being made is different. Instead of collecting and arranging details into a single, synthesized story, the task is to abstract away from the specific details of individual papers and to find the common threads that unite them and make sense of the document collection as a whole.

Another challenge with summarization of scientific literature becomes clear as one compares alternative reviews of the same literature. Each review author brings their own unique perspective and questions to bear in their reading and presentation of that literature. While this is true of other genres of documents that have been the target of multi-document summarization work in the past, we don't find query oriented approaches to multi-document summarization of scientific articles. One contribution of this work is a technical approach to query oriented multi-document summarization of scientific articles that has been evaluated in comparison with a competitive baseline that is not query oriented. The evaluation demonstrates the advantage of the query oriented approach for this type of summarization.

We present a system called SciSumm that summarizes document collections that are composed of lists of papers cited together within the same source article, otherwise known as a co-citation. Using the context of the co-citation in the source article, we generate a query that allows us to generate a summary in a query-oriented fashion. The extracted por-

Proceedings of the Workshop on Automatic Summarization for Different Genres, Media, and Languages, pages 8–15,
Portland, Oregon, June 23, 2011.

tions of the co-cited articles are then assembled into clusters that represent the main themes of the articles that relate to the context in which they were cited. Our evaluation demonstrates that SciSumm achieves higher quality summaries than the MEAD summarization system (Radev, 2004).

The rest of the paper is organized as follows. We present an overview of relevant literature in Section 2. The end-to-end summarization pipeline has been described in Section 3 . Section 4 presents an evaluation of summaries generated from the system. We end the paper with conclusions and some interesting further research directions in Section 5.

2 Literature Review

We begin our literature review by thinking about some common use cases for multi-document summarization of scientific articles.

First consider that as a researcher reads a scientific article, she/he encounters numerous citations, most of them citing the foundational and seminal work that is important in that scientific domain. The text surrounding these citations is a valuable resource as it allows the author to make a statement about her viewpoint towards the cited articles. A tool that could provide a small summary of the collection of cited articles that is constructed specifically to relate to the claims made by the author citing them would be useful. It might also help the researcher determine if the cited work is relevant for her own research.

As an example of such a co-citation consider the following citation sentence

Various machine learning approaches have been proposed for chunking (Ramshaw and Marcus, 1995; Tjong Kim Sang, 2000a; Tjong Kim Sang et al. , 2000; Tjong Kim Sang, 2000b; Sassano and Utsuro, 2000; van Halteren, 2000).

Now imagine the reader trying to determine about widely used *machine learning* approaches for *noun phrase chunking*. Instead of going through these individual papers, it would be more useful to get the summary of the topics in all those papers that talk about the usage of machine learning methods in chunking.

2.1 Overview of Multi-Document Summarization

An exhaustive summary of recent work in summarization is out of the scope for this paper. Hence, we review only the most relevant approaches in summarization to our current work. As most recent work in multi-document summarization has been extractive, and in our observation, scientific articles contain the type of information that we would want in a summary, we follow this convention. This allows us to avoid the complexities of natural language generation based approaches in abstractive summarization.

Multi-document summarization is an extension of single document summarization in which the thematically important textual fragments are extracted from multiple comparable documents, e.g., news articles describing the same event. The techniques not only need to address identification and removal of redundant information but also inclusion of unique and novel contributions. Various graph based (Mani et al., 1997) and centroid clustering based methods (Radev et al., 2000) have been proposed to address the problem of multi-document summarization. Both of these methods identify common themes present in a document collection using a sentence similarity metric.

2.2 Summarization of Scientific Articles

Surprisingly, not many approaches to the problem of summarization of scientific articles have been proposed in the past. One exception is Teufel and Moens (2002), who view summarization as a classification task in which they use a Naive Bayes classifier to assign a rhetorical status to each sentence in an article and thus divide the whole article into regions with a specific argumentation status (e.g. categories such as AIM, CONTRAST and BACKGROUND). In our proposed approach, we are trying to identify reoccurring topic themes that are common across the articles and may appear under a variety of rhetorical headings.

Nanba and colleagues (1999) argue in their work that a co-citation frequently implies a consistent viewpoint towards the cited articles. Similarly, for articles cited within different sentences, textual similarity between the articles is inversely proportional to the size of the sentential gap between the citations.

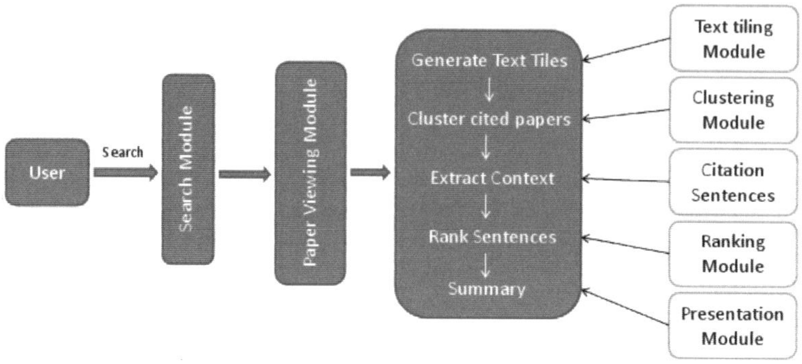

Figure 1: SciSumm summarization pipeline

In our work we make use of this insight by generating a query to focus our multi-document summary from the text closest to the citation. Qazvinian and colleagues (2008) present a summarization approach that can be seen as the converse of what we are working to achieve. Rather than summarizing multiple papers cited in the same source article, they summarize different viewpoints expressed towards the same article from different citing articles. Some of the insights they use in their work also apply to our problem. They used a clustering approach over different citations for the same target article for discovery of different ways of thinking about that article. Citation text has been already shown to contain important concepts about the article that might be absent from other important sections of an article e.g. an *Abstract* (Mohammad et al., 2009) . Template based generation of summaries possessing similar hierarchical topic structure as the *Related Work* section in an article has also been proposed (Hoang et al., 2010). In our work, we consider a flat topic structure in the form of topic clusters. More specifically, we discover the comparable attributes of the co-cited articles using Frequent Term Based Clustering (Beil et al., 2002). The clusters generated in this process contain a set of topically related text fragments called tiles, which are extracted from the set of co-cited articles. Each cluster is indexed with a label, which is a frequent term set present in the tile. We take this to be an approximation of a description for the topic represented by the cluster.

3 System Overview of the SciSumm Summarization System

A high level overview of our system's architecture is presented in Figure 1 . The system provides a web based interface for viewing and summarizing research articles in the ACL Anthology corpus, 2008. The summarization proceeds in three main stages. First, a user may retrieve a collection of articles of interest by entering a query. SciSumm responds by returning a list of relevant articles. The user can continue to read an article of interest as shown in Figure 2. The co-citations in the paper are highlighted in bold and italics to mark them as points of interest for the user. If a user clicks on a co-citation, SciSumm responds by generating a query from the local context of the co-citation and uses it to rank the clusters generated.

As an example consider the following citation sentence "Various machine learning approaches have been proposed for chunking (Ramshaw and Marcus, 1995; Tjong Kim Sang, 2000a; Tjong Kim Sang et al. , 2000; Tjong Kim Sang, 2000b; Sassano and Utsuro, 2000; van Halteren, 2000)". If the user clicks on this co-citation, SciSumm generates a list of clusters and ranks them for relevance. Most of the top ranked cluster labels thus generated are shown in Figure 3 along with the cluster content of the highest ranked cluster labelled as *Phrase, Noun*. The labels index into the corresponding cluster. An example of such cluster is displayed in Figure 4. The cluster has a label *Chunk* and contains tiles from two of the three papers discussing about a topic identi-

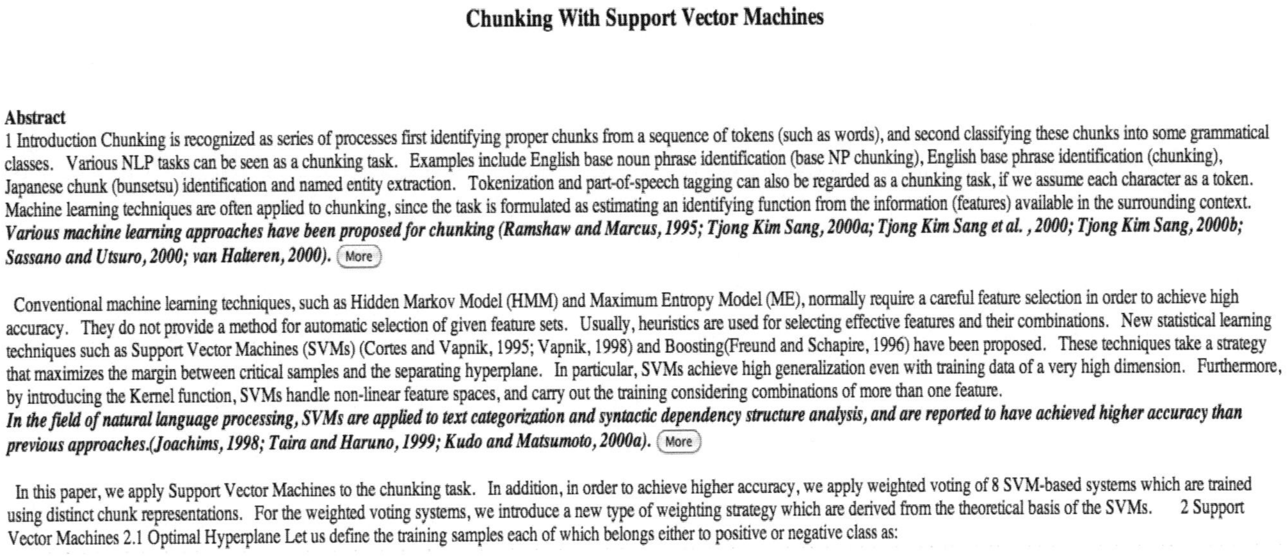

Chunking With Support Vector Machines

Abstract
1 Introduction Chunking is recognized as series of processes first identifying proper chunks from a sequence of tokens (such as words), and second classifying these chunks into some grammatical classes. Various NLP tasks can be seen as a chunking task. Examples include English base noun phrase identification (base NP chunking), English base phrase identification (chunking), Japanese chunk (bunsetsu) identification and named entity extraction. Tokenization and part-of-speech tagging can also be regarded as a chunking task, if we assume each character as a token. Machine learning techniques are often applied to chunking, since the task is formulated as estimating an identifying function from the information (features) available in the surrounding context. ***Various machine learning approaches have been proposed for chunking (Ramshaw and Marcus, 1995; Tjong Kim Sang, 2000a; Tjong Kim Sang et al. , 2000; Tjong Kim Sang, 2000b; Sassano and Utsuro, 2000; van Halteren, 2000).*** More

Conventional machine learning techniques, such as Hidden Markov Model (HMM) and Maximum Entropy Model (ME), normally require a careful feature selection in order to achieve high accuracy. They do not provide a method for automatic selection of given feature sets. Usually, heuristics are used for selecting effective features and their combinations. New statistical learning techniques such as Support Vector Machines (SVMs) (Cortes and Vapnik, 1995; Vapnik, 1998) and Boosting(Freund and Schapire, 1996) have been proposed. These techniques take a strategy that maximizes the margin between critical samples and the separating hyperplane. In particular, SVMs achieve high generalization even with training data of a very high dimension. Furthermore, by introducing the Kernel function, SVMs handle non-linear feature spaces, and carry out the training considering combinations of more than one feature. ***In the field of natural language processing, SVMs are applied to text categorization and syntactic dependency structure analysis, and are reported to have achieved higher accuracy than previous approaches.(Joachims, 1998; Taira and Haruno, 1999; Kudo and Matsumoto, 2000a).*** More

In this paper, we apply Support Vector Machines to the chunking task. In addition, in order to achieve higher accuracy, we apply weighted voting of 8 SVM-based systems which are trained using distinct chunk representations. For the weighted voting systems, we introduce a new type of weighting strategy which are derived from the theoretical basis of the SVMs. 2 Support Vector Machines 2.1 Optimal Hyperplane Let us define the training samples each of which belongs either to positive or negative class as:

Figure 2: Interface to read a paper. The sentences containing co-citations are automatically highlighted and contain a "More" button beside them letting the user elaborate on the sentence.

fied by this label. In this specific example the topic was not shared by tiles present in the third paper. The words highlighted are interesting terms which are either part of the label of the cluster or show a low IDF (Inverse Document Frequency) amongst the tiles generated from the co-cited papers. These words are presented as hyper-links to the search interface and can be further used as search queries for finding articles on related topics.

3.1 System Description

SciSumm has four primary modules that are central to the functionality of the system, as displayed in Figure 1. First, the Text Tiling module takes care of obtaining tiles of text relevant to the citation context. It uses the Texttiling algorithm (Hearst, 1997), to segment the co-cited papers into text tiles based on topic shifts identified using a term overlap measure computed between fixed-length blocks of text. Next, the clustering module is used to generate labelled clusters using the text tiles extracted from the co-cited papers. The labels provide a conveniently comprehensible and yet terse description of each cluster. We have used a Frequent Term Based Clustering algorithm (Beil et al., 2002) for clustering. The clusters are ordered according to relevance with respect to the generated query. This is accomplished by the Ranking Module. Finally, the summary presentation module is used to display the ranked clusters obtained from the ranking module. Alongside the clusters, an HTML pane also shows the labels of all the clusters. Having such a bird's-eye view of all the cluster labels helps the user to quickly navigate to an interesting topic. The entire pipeline is used in real-time to generate topic clusters which are useful for generating snippet summary and more exploratory analysis.

In the following sections, we discuss each of the main modules in detail.

3.2 Texttiling

The Text Tiling module uses the TextTiling algorithm (Hearst, 1997) for segmenting the text of each article. Each such segment obtained by the TextTiling algorithm has been referred as a text tile. We have used these text tiles as the basic unit for our summary since individual sentences are too short to stand on their own. Once computed, text tiles are used to identify the context associated with a co-citation. The intuition is that an embedded co-citation in a text tile is connected with the topic distribution of the tile. We use important text from this tile to rank the text clusters generated using Frequent Term based text clustering.

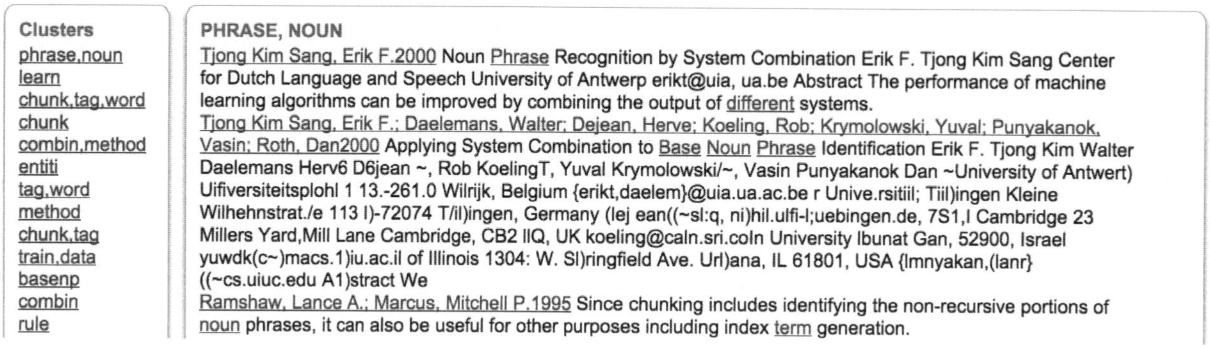

Figure 3: Clusters generated in response to a user click on the co-citation. The list of clusters in the left pane gives a bird-eye view of the topics which are present in the co-cited papers

3.3 Frequent Term Based Clustering

The clustering module employs Frequent Term Based Clustering (Beil et al., 2002). For each co-citation, we use this clustering technique to cluster all the of the extracted text tiles generated by segmenting each of the co-cited papers. We settled on this clustering approach for the following reasons:

- Text tile contents coming from different papers constitute a sparse vector space, and thus the centroid based approaches would not work very well.
- Frequent Term based clustering is extremely fast in execution time as well as and relatively efficient in terms of space requirements.
- A frequent term set is generated for each cluster which gives a comprehensible description of the cluster.

Frequent Term Based text clustering uses a group of frequently co-occurring terms called a frequent term set. Each frequent term set indexes to a corresponding cluster. The frequent term set has the property that it occurs at least once in each of the documents present in the cluster. The algorithm uses the first *k* term sets if all the documents in the document collections are clustered.To discover all the possible candidates for clustering, i.e., term sets, we used the *Apriori* algorithm (Agrawal et al., 1994), which identifies the sets of terms that are relatively frequent. We use entropy measure to score each frequent term set as discovered from the Apriori algorithm. The entropy overlap of a cluster C_i, $EO(C_i)$ is calculated as follows:

$$EO(C_i) = \sum_{D_j \epsilon C_i} -\frac{1}{f_j}.ln(\frac{1}{f_j})$$

where D_j is the jth document which gets binned in the cluster C_i, f_j is the number of clusters which contain D_j. A smaller value means that the document D_j is contained in few other clusters C_i. $EO(C_i)$ increases monotonically as f_j increases. We thus rank the clusters with their corresponding $EO(C_i)$ and then pick a cluster with the smallest entropy overlap $EO(C_i)$. Once a cluster is chosen to be included in the final clustering, we remove the documents present in chosen cluster from other candidate clusters. This results in a hard clustering of documents. We also remove term set corresponding to C_i from the list of candidate frequent term sets and then again recompute the $EO(C_i)$'s for the clusters. We continue this re-scoring and selecting a candidate cluster until the final clustering does not completely exhaust the entire document collection.

3.4 Cluster Ranking

The ranking module uses cosine similarity between the query and the centroid of each cluster to rank all the clusters generated by the clustering module. The context of a co-citation is restricted to the text of the tile in which the co-citation is found. In this way we attempt to leverage the expert knowledge of the author as it is encoded in the local context of the co-citation in our process of automatically ranking the clusters in terms of importance.

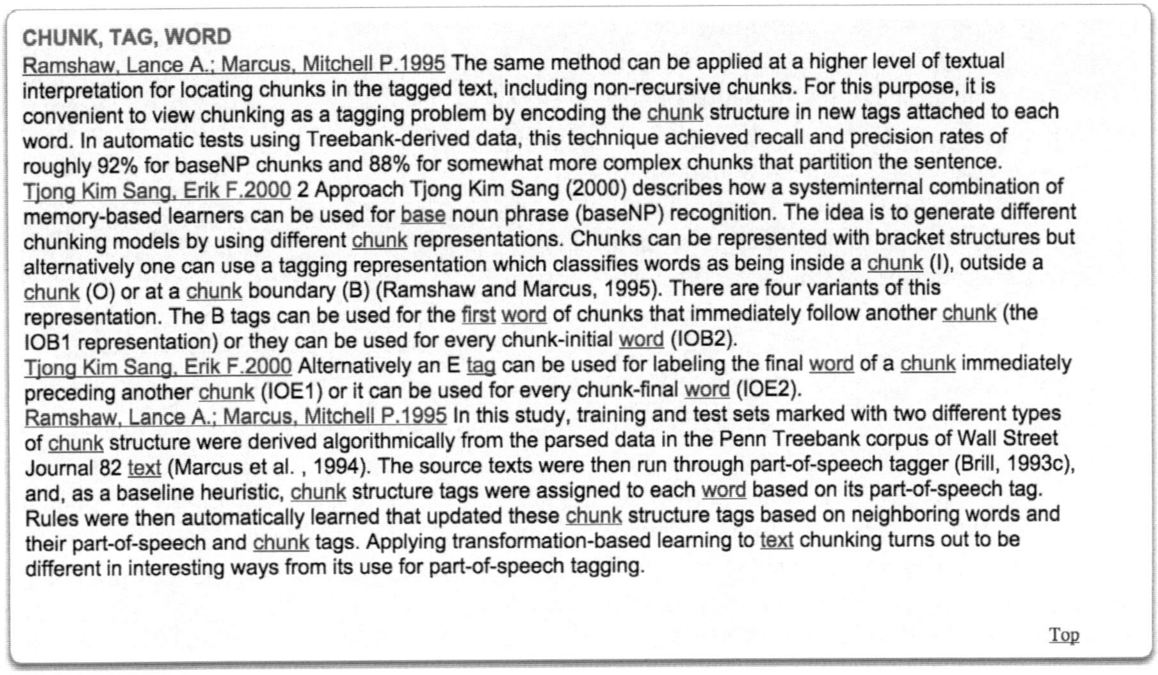

CHUNK, TAG, WORD

Ramshaw, Lance A.; Marcus, Mitchell P.1995 The same method can be applied at a higher level of textual interpretation for locating chunks in the tagged text, including non-recursive chunks. For this purpose, it is convenient to view chunking as a tagging problem by encoding the chunk structure in new tags attached to each word. In automatic tests using Treebank-derived data, this technique achieved recall and precision rates of roughly 92% for baseNP chunks and 88% for somewhat more complex chunks that partition the sentence.
Tjong Kim Sang, Erik F.2000 2 Approach Tjong Kim Sang (2000) describes how a systeminternal combination of memory-based learners can be used for base noun phrase (baseNP) recognition. The idea is to generate different chunking models by using different chunk representations. Chunks can be represented with bracket structures but alternatively one can use a tagging representation which classifies words as being inside a chunk (I), outside a chunk (O) or at a chunk boundary (B) (Ramshaw and Marcus, 1995). There are four variants of this representation. The B tags can be used for the first word of chunks that immediately follow another chunk (the IOB1 representation) or they can be used for every chunk-initial word (IOB2).
Tjong Kim Sang, Erik F.2000 Alternatively an E tag can be used for labeling the final word of a chunk immediately preceding another chunk (IOE1) or it can be used for every chunk-final word (IOE2).
Ramshaw, Lance A.; Marcus, Mitchell P.1995 In this study, training and test sets marked with two different types of chunk structure were derived algorithmically from the parsed data in the Penn Treebank corpus of Wall Street Journal 82 text (Marcus et al. , 1994). The source texts were then run through part-of-speech tagger (Brill, 1993c), and, as a baseline heuristic, chunk structure tags were assigned to each word based on its part-of-speech tag. Rules were then automatically learned that updated these chunk structure tags based on neighboring words and their part-of-speech and chunk tags. Applying transformation-based learning to text chunking turns out to be different in interesting ways from its use for part-of-speech tagging.

Top

Figure 4: Example of a summary generated by our system. We can see that the clusters are cross cutting across different papers, thus giving the user a multi-document summary.

4 Evaluation

In a typical evaluation of a multi-document summarization system, gold standard summaries are evaluated against fixed length generated summaries. Summarization conferences such as DUC have competitions where different summarization systems compete on a standard task of generating summaries for a publicly available dataset. The summaries generated using each individual summarization system are then evaluated against the summaries prepared by human annotators. Summarization of scientific article is a novel task and hence no test collection of gold standard summaries exist. Thus, it was necessary to prepare our own evaluation corpus, consisting of gold standard multi-document summaries for a set of randomly selected co-citations.

4.1 Experimental Setup

An important target user population for multi-document summarization of scientific articles is graduate students. Hence to get a measure of how well the summarization system is performing, we asked 2 graduate students who have been working in the computational linguistics community to create gold standard summaries of a fixed length (8 sentences $\sim$ 200 words) for ten different randomly selected co-citations. The students were given guidelines to prepare summaries based on the design goals of the SciSumm system, but not any of its technical details. Thus, for 10 co-citations, we obtained two different gold standard summaries. For ROUGE-1 the average score between each pair of gold standard summaries was 0.518 (Min = 0.388, Max = 0.686). Similarly for ROUGE-2 the average score was 0.242 (Min = 0.119, Max=0.443). While these scores do not have a well-calibrated meaning to them, they give an indication of the complexity of the task. Since the annotators were creating extractive summaries which could justify the co-citation, they had to pay special attention to the section where the co-citation came from. One can consider this similar to the sense making process a reader might go through when using the citing paper as a lens through which to interpret the cited literature.

Note that while SciSumm provides users with an interactive interface that supports navigation between documents, the gold standard summaries are static. Thus, our evaluation is designed to measure the quality of the content selection when taking into consideration the citation context. This would also help us to evaluate the influence exerted by the citation context in the gold standard summaries. In future work, we will evaluate the usability of the SciSumm system using a task based evaluation.

In the absence of any other multi-document summarization systems in the domain of scientific article summarization, we used a widely used and freely available multi-document summarization system called MEAD (Radev, 2004) as our baseline. MEAD uses centroid based summarization to create informative clusters of topics. We use the default configuration of MEAD in which MEAD uses length, position and centroid for ranking each sentence. We did not use query focussed summarization with MEAD. We evaluate its performance with the same gold standard summaries we use to evaluate SciSumm. For generating a summary from our system we used sentences from the tiles which gets clustered in the top ranked cluster. When that entire cluster is exhausted we move on to the next highly ranked cluster. In this way we prepare a summary comprising of 8 sentences.

4.2 Results

For measuring performance of the two summarization systems (SciSumm and MEAD), we compute the ROUGE metric based on the 2 * 10 gold standard summaries that were manually created. ROUGE has been traditionally used to compute the performance based on the N-gram overlap (ROUGE-N) between the summaries generated by the system and the target gold summaries. For our evaluation we used two different versions of the ROUGE metric, namely ROUGE-1 and ROUGE-2, which correspond to measures of the unigram and bigram overlap respectively. We computed four metrics in order to measure SciSumm's performance, namely ROUGE-1 F-measure, ROUGE-1 Recall, ROUGE-2 F-measure, and ROUGE-2 Recall. To measure the statistical significance of this result, we carried out a Student T-Test, the results of which are presented in the results section. The t-test results displayed in Table 1 show that our systems performs significantly better than MEAD on three of the metrics ($p < .05$). On two additional metrics, SciSumm performs marginally better ($p < .1$).

This shows that using the query generated out of the co-citation is useful for content selection

Table 1: Average ROUGE results. * represents improvement significant at $p < .05$, † at $p < .01$.

Metric	MEAD	SciSumm
ROUGE-1 F-measure	0.3680	0.5123 †
ROUGE-1 Recall	0.4168	0.5018
ROUGE-1 Precision	0.3424	0.5349 †
ROUGE-2 F-measure	0.1598	0.3303 *
ROUGE-2 Recall	0.1786	0.3227 *
ROUGE-2 Precision	0.1481	0.3450 †

from cited papers. Intuitively, this makes sense as each researcher would have a unique perspective when reviewing scientific literature. Co-citations can be considered as micro-reviews which summarizes the thread unifying the research presented in each of the cited papers. This provides evidence that the co-citation context provides useful information for forming an effective query to focus the multi-document summary to reflect the perspective of the author of the citing paper.

5 Conclusions and Future Work

In this work, we proposed the first unsupervised approach to the problem of multi-document summarization of scientific articles that we know of. In this approach, the document collection is a list of papers cited together within the same source article, otherwise known as a co-citation. The summary is presented in the form of topic labeled clusters, which provide easy navigation based on the user's topic of interest. Another contribution is a technical approach to query oriented multi-document summarization of scientific articles that has been evaluated in comparison with a competitive baseline that is not query oriented. Our evaluation shows that the SciSumm approach to content selection outperforms another multi-document summarization system for this summarization task.

Our long term goal is to expand the capabilities of SciSumm to generate literature surveys of larger document collections from less focused queries. This more challenging task would require more control over filtering and ranking in order to avoid generating summaries that lack focus. To this end, a future improvement that we plan to use a variant on MMR (Maximum Marginal Relevance) (Carbonell et al., 1998), which can be used to optimize the diversity of selected text tiles as well as the relevance based ordering of clusters in order to put a more diverse set of observations from the co-cited articles at the fingertips of users. A natural extension would also be to discover the nature of citations to generate improved summaries. Non-explicit citations (Qazvinian et al., 2010) which could be used to generate similar topic clusters.

Another important direction is to refine the interaction design through task-based user studies. As we collect more feedback from students and researchers through this process, we will use the insights gained to achieve a more robust and effective implementation. We also plan to leverage research in information visualization to enhance the usability of the system.

6 Acknowledgements

This work was supported by NSF EEC-064848 and NSF EEC-0935127.

References

Agrawal R. and Srikant R. 1994. Fast Algorithm for Mining Association Rules In *Proceedings of the 20th VLDB Conference* Santiago, Chile, 1994

Baxendale, P. 1958. Machine-made index for technical literature - an experiment. *IBM Journal of Research and Development*

Beil F., Ester M. and Xu X 2002. Frequent-Term based Text Clustering In *Proceedings of SIGKDD '02* Edmonton, Alberta, Canada

Carbonell J. and Goldstein J. 1998. The Use of MMR, Diversity-Based Reranking for Reordering Documents and Producing Summaries In *Research and Development in Information Retrieval*, pages 335–336

Councill I. G. , Giles C. L. and Kan M. 2008. ParsCit: An open-source CRF reference string parsing package *INTERNATIONAL LANGUAGE RESOURCES AND EVALUATION European Language Resources Association*

Edmundson, H.P. 1969. New methods in automatic extracting. *Journal of ACM.*

Hearst M.A. 1997 TextTiling: Segmenting text into multi-paragraph subtopic passages *In proceedings of LREC 2004, Lisbon, Portugal, May 2004*

Joseph M. T. and Radev D. R. 2007. Citation analysis, centrality, and the ACL Anthology

Kupiec J. , Pedersen J. , Chen F. 1995. A training document summarizer. In *Proceedings SIGIR '95*, pages 68-73, New York, NY, USA. 28(1):114–133.

Luhn, H. P. 1958. *IBM Journal of Research Development.*

Mani I. , Bloedorn E. 1997. Multi-Document Summarization by graph search and matching In *AAAI/IAAI*, pages 622-628. [15, 16].

Nanba H. , Okumura M. 1999. Towards Multi-paper Summarization Using Reference Information In *Proceedings of IJCAI-99*, pages 926–931 .

Paice CD. 1990. Constructing Literature Abstracts by Computer: Techniques and Prospects *Information Processing and Management* Vol. 26, No.1, pp, 171-186, 1990

Qazvinian V. , Radev D.R 2008. Scientific Paper summarization using Citation Summary Networks In *Proceedings of the 22nd International Conference on Computational Linguistics*, pages 689–696 Manchester, August 2008

Radev D. R . , Jing H. and Budzikowska M. 2000. Centroid-based summarization of multiple documents: sentence extraction, utility based evaluation, and user studies In *NAACL-ANLP 2000 Workshop on Automatic summarization*, pages 21-30, Morristown, NJ, USA. [12, 16, 17].

Radev, Dragomir. 2004. *MEAD - a platform for multi-document multilingual text summarization.* In proceedings of LREC 2004, Lisbon, Portugal, May 2004.

Teufel S. , Moens M. 2002. Summarizing Scientific Articles - Experiments with Relevance and Rhetorical Status In *Journal of Computational Linguistics*, MIT Press.

Mohammad, Saif and Dorr, Bonnie and Egan, Melissa and Hassan, Ahmed and Muthukrishan, Pradeep and Qazvinian, Vahed and Radev, Dragomir and Zajic, David 2009. Using citations to generate surveys of scientific paradigms In *Proceedings of Human Language Technologies:The 2009 Annual Conference of the North American Chapter of the Association for Computational Linguistics*

Qazvinian, Vahed and Radev, Dragomir R. 2010. Identifying non-explicit citing sentences for citation-based summarization In *Proceedings of the 48th Annual Meeting of the Association for Computational Linguistics*

Hoang, Cong Duy Vu and Kan, Min-Yen 2010. Towards automated related work summarization In *Proceedings of the 23rd International Conference on Computational Linguistics: Posters*

Summarizing Decisions in Spoken Meetings

Lu Wang
Department of Computer Science
Cornell University
Ithaca, NY 14853
luwang@cs.cornell.edu

Claire Cardie
Department of Computer Science
Cornell University
Ithaca, NY 14853
cardie@cs.cornell.edu

Abstract

This paper addresses the problem of summarizing decisions in spoken meetings: our goal is to produce a concise *decision abstract* for each meeting decision. We explore and compare token-level and dialogue act-level automatic summarization methods using both unsupervised and supervised learning frameworks. In the supervised summarization setting, and given true clusterings of decision-related utterances, we find that token-level summaries that employ discourse context can approach an upper bound for decision abstracts derived directly from dialogue acts. In the unsupervised summarization setting,we find that summaries based on unsupervised partitioning of decision-related utterances perform comparably to those based on partitions generated using supervised techniques (0.22 ROUGE-F1 using LDA-based topic models vs. 0.23 using SVMs).

1 Introduction

Meetings are a common way for people to share information and discuss problems. And an effective meeting always leads to concrete decisions. As a result, it would be useful to develop automatic methods that summarize not the entire meeting dialogue, but just the important decisions made. In particular, decision summaries would allow participants to review decisions from previous meetings as they prepare for an upcoming meeting. For those who did not participate in the earlier meetings, decision summaries might provide one type of efficient overview of the meeting contents. For managers, decision summaries could act as a concise record of the idea generation process.

While there has been some previous work in summarizing meetings and conversations, very little work has focused on decision summarization: Fernández et al. (2008a) and Bui et al. (2009) investigate the use of a semantic parser and machine learning methods for phrase- and token-level decision summarization. We believe our work is the first to explore and compare token-level and dialogue act-level approaches — using both unsupervised and supervised learning methods — for summarizing decisions in meetings.

C: Just spinning and not scrolling , I would say . (1)
C: But if you've got a [disfmarker] if if you've got a flipped thing , effectively it's something that's curved on one side and flat on the other side , but you folded it in half . (2)
D: the case would be rubber and the the buttons , (3)
B: I think the spinning wheel is definitely very now . (1)
B: and then make the colour of the main remote [vocal-sound] the colour like vegetable colours , do you know ? (4)
B: I mean I suppose vegetable colours would be orange and green and some reds and um maybe purple (4)
A: but since LCDs seems to be uh a definite yes , (1)
A: Flat on the top . (2)
Decision Abstracts (Summary)
DECISION 1: The remote will have an LCD and spinning wheel inside.
DECISION 2: The case will be flat on top and curved on the bottom.
DECISION 3: The remote control and its buttons will be made of rubber.
DECISION 4: The remote will resemble a vegetable and be in bright vegetable colors.

Table 1: A clip of a meeting from the AMI meeting corpus (Carletta et al., 2005). A, B, C and D refer to distinct speakers; the numbers in parentheses indicate the associated meeting decision: DECISION 1, 2, 3 or 4. Also shown is the gold-standard (manual) abstract (summary) for each decision.

Proceedings of the Workshop on Automatic Summarization for Different Genres, Media, and Languages, pages 16–24,
Portland, Oregon, June 23, 2011.

Consider the sample dialogue snippet in Table 1, which is part of the AMI meeting corpus (Carletta et al., 2005). The Table lists only *decision-related dialogue acts (DRDAs)* — utterances associated with at least one decision made in the meeting.[1] The DRDAs are ordered by time; intervening utterances are not shown. DRDAs are important because they contain critical information for decision summary construction.

Table 1 clearly shows some challenges for decision summarization for spoken meetings beyond the disfluencies, high word error rates, absence of punctuation, interruptions and hesitations due to speech. First, different decisions can be discussed more or less concurrently; as a result, *the utterances associated with a single decision are not contiguous in the dialogue*. In Table 1, the dialogue acts (henceforth, DAs) concerning DECISION 1, for example, are interleaved with DAs for other decisions. Second, *some decision-related DAs contribute more than others to the associated decision*. In composing the summary for DECISION 1, for example, we might safely ignore the first DA for DECISION 1. Finally, more so than for standard text summarization, *purely extract-based summaries are not likely to be easily interpretable*: DRDAs often contain text that is irrelevant to the decision and many will only be understandable if analyzed in the context of the surrounding utterances.

In this paper, we study methods for decision summarization for spoken meetings. We assume that all decision-related DAs have been identified and aim to produce a summary for the meeting in the form of concise *decision abstracts* (see Table 1), one for each decision made. In response to the challenges described above, we propose a summarization framework that includes:

Clustering of decision-related DAs. Here we aim to partition the decision-related utterances (DRDAs) according to the decisions each supports. This step is similar in spirit to many standard text summarization techniques (Salton et al., 1997) that begin by grouping sentences according to semantic similarity.

Summarization at the DA-level. We select just the important DRDAs in each cluster. Our goal is to eliminate redundant and less informative utterances. The selected DRDAs are then concatenated to form the decision summary.

Optional token-level summarization of the selected DRDAs. Methods are employed to capture concisely the gist of each decision, discarding any distracting text.

Incorporation of the discourse context as needed. We hypothesize that this will produce more interpretable summaries.

More specifically, we compare both unsupervised (TFIDF (Salton et al., 1997) and LDA topic modeling (Blei et al., 2003)) and (pairwise) supervised clustering procedures (using SVMs and MaxEnt) for partitioning DRDAs according to the decision each supports. We also investigate unsupervised methods and supervised learning for decision summarization at both the DA and token level, with and without the incorporation of discourse context. During training, the supervised decision summarizers are told which DRDAs for each decision are the most informative for constructing the decision abstract.

Our experiments employ the aforementioned AMI meeting corpus: we compare our decision summaries to the manually generated decision abstracts for each meeting and evaluate performance using the ROUGE-1 (Lin and Hovy, 2003) text summarization evaluation metric.

In the supervised summarization setting, our experiments demonstrate that with true clusterings of decision-related DAs, token-level summaries that employ limited discourse context can approach an upper bound for summaries extracted directly from DRDAs[2] — 0.4387 ROUGE-F1 vs. 0.5333. When using system-generated DRDA clusterings, the DA-level summaries always dominate token-level methods in terms of performance.

For the unsupervised summarization setting, we investigate the use of both unsupervised and supervised methods for the initial DRDA clustering step. We find that summaries based on unsupervised clusterings perform comparably to those generated using supervised techniques (0.2214 ROUGE-F1 using LDA-based topic models vs. 0.2349 using SVMs). As in the supervised summarization setting, we observe that including additional discourse context boosts performance only for token-level summaries.

[1]These are similar, but not completely equivalent, to the *decision dialogue acts (DDAs)* of Bui et al. (2009), Fernández et al. (2008a), Frampton et al. (2009). The latter refer to all DAs that appear in a decision discussion even if they do NOT support any particular decision.

[2]The upper bound measures the vocabulary overlap of each gold-standard decision summary with the complete text of all of its associated DRDAs.

2 Related Work

There exists much previous research on automatic text summarization using corpus-based, knowledge-based or statistical methods (Mani, 1999; Marcu, 2000). Dialogue summarization methods, however, generally try to account for the special characteristics of speech. Among early work in this subarea, Zechner (2002) investigates speech summarization based on maximal marginal relevance (MMR) and cross-speaker linking of information. Popular supervised methods for summarizing speech — including maximum entropy, conditional random fields (CRFs), and support vector machines (SVMs) — are investigated in Buist et al. (2004), Xie et al. (2008) and Galley (2006). Techniques for determining semantic similarity are used for selecting relevant utterances in Gurevych and Strube (2004).

Studies in Banerjee et al. (2005) show that decisions are considered to be one of the most important outputs of meetings. And in recent years, there has been much research on detecting decision-related DAs. Hsueh and Moore (2008), for example, propose maximum entropy classification techniques to identify DRDAs in meetings; Fernández et al. (2008b) develop a model of decision-making dialogue structure and detect decision DAs based on it; and Frampton et al. (2009) implement a real-time decision detection system.

Fernández et al. (2008a) and Bui et al. (2009), however, might be the most relevant previous work to ours. The systems in both papers run an open-domain semantic parser on meeting transcriptions to produce multiple short fragments, and then employ machine learning methods to select the phrases or words that comprise the decision summary. Although their task is also decision summarization, their gold-standard summaries consist of manually annotated words from the meeting while we judge performance using manually constructed decision abstracts as the gold standard. The latter are more readable, but often use a vocabulary different from that of the associated decision-related utterances in the meeting.

Our work differs from all of the above in that we (1) incorporate a clustering step to partition DRDAs according to the decision each supports; (2) generate decision summaries at both the DA- and token-level; and (3) investigate the role of discourse context for decision summarization.

In the following sections, we investigate methods for clustering DRDAs (Section 3) and generating DA-level and token-level decision summaries (Section 4). In each case, we evaluate the methods using the AMI meeting corpus.

3 Clustering Decision-Related Dialogue Acts

We design a preprocessing step that facilitates decision summarization by clustering all of the decision-related dialogue acts according to the decision(s) it supports. Because it is not clear how many decisions are made in a meeting, we use a hierarchical agglomerative clustering algorithm (rather than techniques that require *a priori* knowledge of the number of clusters) and choose the proper stopping conditions. In particular, we employ *average-link* methods: at each iteration, we merge the two clusters with the maximum average pairwise similarity among their DRDAs. In the following subsections, we introduce unsupervised and supervised methods for measuring the pairwise DRDA similarity.

3.1 DRDA Similarity: Unsupervised Methods

We consider two unsupervised similarity measures — one based on the TF-IDF score from the Information Retrieval research community, and a second based on Latent Dirichlet Allocation topic models.

TF-IDF similarity. TF-IDF similarity metrics have worked well as a measure of document similarity. As a result, we employ it as one metric for measuring the similarity of two DRDAs. Suppose there are L distinct word types in the corpus. We treat each decision-related dialgue act DA_i as a document, and represent it as an L-dimensional feature vector $\overrightarrow{FV_i} = (x_{i1}, x_{i2}, ..., x_{iL})$, where x_{ik} is word w_k's $tf \cdot idf$ score for DA_i. Then the (average-link) similarity of cluster C_m and cluster C_n, $Sim\_TFIDF(C_m, C_n)$, is defined as :

$$\frac{1}{\mid C_m \mid \cdot \mid C_n \mid} \sum_{\substack{DA_i \in C_m \\ DA_j \in C_n}} \frac{\overrightarrow{FV_i} \cdot \overrightarrow{FV_j}}{\parallel \overrightarrow{FV_i} \parallel \parallel \overrightarrow{FV_j} \parallel}$$

LDA topic models. In recent years, topic models have become a popular technique for discovering the latent structure of "topics" or "concepts" in a corpus. Here we use the Latent Dirichlet Allocation (LDA) topic models of Blei et al. (2003) — unsuper-

Features
number of overlapping words
proportion of the number of overlapping words to the length of shorter DA
TF-IDF similarity
whether the DAs are in an adjacency pair (see 4.3)
time difference of pairwise DAs
relative dialogue position of pairwise DAs
whether the two DAs have the same DA type
number of overlapping words in the contexts (see 4.2)

Table 2: Features for Pairwise Supervised Clustering

vised probabilistic generative models that estimate the properties of multinomial observations. In our setting, LDA-based topic models provide a soft clustering of the DRDAs according to the topics they discuss.[3] To determine the similarity of two DRDAs, we effectively measure the similarity of their term-based topic distributions.

To train an LDA-based topic model for our task[4], we treat each DRDA as an individual document. After training, each DRDA, DA_i, is assigned a topic distribution $\overrightarrow{\theta_i}$ according to the learned model. Thus, we can define the similarity of cluster C_m and cluster C_n, $Sim\_LDA(C_m, C_n)$, as :

$$\frac{1}{\mid C_m \mid \cdot \mid C_n \mid} \sum_{\substack{DA_i \in C_m \\ DA_j \in C_n}} \overrightarrow{\theta_i} \cdot \overrightarrow{\theta_j}$$

3.2 DRDA Similarity: Supervised Techniques

In addition to unsupervised methods for clustering DRDAs, we also explore an approach based on *Pairwise Supervised Learning*: we develop a classifier that determines whether or not a pair of DRDAs supports the same decision. So each training and test example is a feature vector that is a function of two DRDAs: for DA_i and DA_j, the feature vector is $\overrightarrow{FV_{ij}} = f(DA_i, DA_j) = \{fv^1_{ij}, fv^2_{ij}, ..., fv^k_{ij}\}$. Table 2 gives a full list of features that are used. Because the annotations for the time information and dialogue type of DAs are available from the corpus, we employ features including time difference of pairwise DAs, relative position[5] and whether they have the same DA type.

We employ Support Vector Machines (SVMs) and Maximum Entropy (MaxEnt) as our learning methods, because SVMs are shown to be effective in text categorization (Joachims, 1998) and MaxEnt has been applied in many natural language processing tasks (Berger et al., 1996). Given an $\overrightarrow{FV_{ij}}$, for SVMs, we utilize the decision value of $\mathbf{w}^T \cdot \overrightarrow{FV_{ij}} + \mathbf{b}$ as the similarity, where $\mathbf{w}$ is the weight vector and $\mathbf{b}$ is the bias. For MaxEnt, we make use of the probability of $P(SameDecision \mid \overrightarrow{FV_{ij}})$ as the similarity value.

3.3 Experiments

Corpus. We use the AMI meeting Corpus (Carletta et al., 2005), a freely available corpus of multiparty meetings that contains a wide range of annotations. The 129 scenario-driven meetings involve four participants playing different roles on a design team. A short (usually one-sentence) abstract is included that describes each decision, action, or problem discussed in the meeting; and each DA is linked to the abstracts it supports. We use the manually constructed decision abstracts as gold-standard summaries and assume that all decision-related DAs have been identified (but not linked to the decision(s) it supports).

Baselines. Two clustering baselines are utilized for comparison. One baseline places all decision-related DAs for the meeting into a single partition (ALLINONEGROUP). The second uses the text segmentation software of Choi (2000) to partition the decision-related DAs (ordered according to time) into several topic-based groups (CHOISEGMENT).

Experimental Setup and Evaluation. Results for pairwise supervised clustering were obtained using 3-fold cross-validation. In the current work, stopping conditions for hierarchical agglomerative clustering are selected manually: For the TF-IDF and topic model approaches, we stop when the similarity measure reaches 0.035 and 0.015, respectively; For the SVM and MaxEnt versions, we use 0 and 0.45, respectively. We use the Mallet implementation for MaxEnt and the SVM^{light} implementation of SVMs.

Our evaluation metrics include b^3 (also called B-cubed) (Bagga and Baldwin, 1998), which is a com-

[3] We cannot easily associate each topic with a decision because the number of decisions is not known *a priori*.

[4] Parameter estimation and inference done by GibbsLDA++.

[5] Here is the definition for the relative position of pairwise DAs. Suppose there are N DAs in one meeting ordered by time, DA_i is the ith DA and DA_j is positioned at j. So the relative position of DA_i and DA_j is $\frac{|i-j|}{N}$.

	B-cubed			Pairwise			VOI
	PRECISION	RECALL	F1	PRECISION	RECALL	F1	
Baselines							
AllInOneGroup	0.2854	1.0000	0.4441	0.1823	1.0000	0.3083	2.2279
ChoiSegment	0.4235	0.9657	0.5888	0.2390	0.8493	0.3730	1.8061
Unsupervised Methods							
TFIDF	0.6840	0.6686	0.6762	0.3281	0.3004	0.3137	1.6604
LDA topic models	0.8265	0.6432	**0.7235**	0.4588	0.2980	**0.3613**	**1.4203**
Pairwise Supervised Methods							
SVM	0.7593	0.7466	**0.7529**	0.5474	0.4821	0.5127	**1.2239**
MaxEnt	0.6999	0.7948	0.7443	0.4858	0.5704	**0.5247**	1.2726

Table 3: Results for Clustering Decision-Related DAs According to the Decision Each Supports

mon measure employed in noun phrase coreference resolution research; a pairwise scorer that measures correctness for every pair of DRDAs; and a variation of information (VOI) scorer (Meilă, 2007), which measures the difference between the distributions of the true clustering and system generated clustering. As space is limited, we refer the readers to the original papers for more details. For b^3 scorer and pairwise scorer, higher results represent better performance; for VOI, lower is better.[6]

Results. The results in Table 3 show first that all of the proposed clustering methods outperform the baselines. Among the unsupervised methods, the LDA topic modeling is preferred to TFIDF. For the supervised methods, SVMs and MaxEnt produce comparable results.

Lexical Features
unigram/bigram
length of the DA
contain digits?
has overlapping words with next DA?
next DA is a positive feedback?
Structural Features
relative position in the meeting?(beginning, ending, or else)
in an AP?
if in an AP, AP type
if in an AP, the other part is decision-related?
if in an AP, is the source part or target part?
if in an AP and is source part, target is positive feedback?
if in an AP and is target part, source is a question?
Discourse Features
relative position to "WRAP UP" or "RECAP"
Other Features
DA type
speaker role
topic

Table 4: Features Used in DA-Level Summarization

4 Decision Summarization

In this section, we turn to decision summarization — extracting a short description of each decision based on the decision-related DAs in each cluster. We investigate options for constructing an extract-based summary that consists of a single DRDA and an abstract-based summary comprised of keywords that describe the decision. For both types of summary, we employ standard techniques from text summarization, but also explore the use of dialogue-specific features and the use of discourse context.

4.1 DA-Level Summarization Based on Unsupervised Methods

We make use of two unsupervised methods to summarize the DRDAs in each "decision cluster". The first method simply returns the longest DRDA in the cluster as the summary (LONGEST DA). The second approach returns the decision cluster prototype, i.e., the DRDA with the largest TF-IDF similarity with the cluster centroid (PROTOTYPE DA). Although important decision-related information may be spread over multiple DRDAs, both unsupervised methods allow us to determine summary quality when summaries are restricted to a single utterance.

4.2 DA-Level and Token-Level Summarization Using Supervised Learning

Because the AMI corpus contains a decision abstract for each decision made in the meeting, we can use this supervisory information to train classifiers that can identify informative DRDAs (for DA-level summaries) or informative tokens (for token-level summaries).

[6]The MUC scorer is popular in coreference evaluation, but it is flawed in measuring the singleton clusters which is prevalent in the AMI corpus. So we do not use it in this work.

Lexical Features
current token/current token and next token length of the DA is digit? appearing in next DA? next DA is a positive feedback?
Structural Features
see Table 3
Grammatical Features
part-of-speech phrase type (VP/NP/PP) dependency relations
Other Features
speaker role topic

Table 5: Features Used in Token-Level Summarization

	PREC	REC	F1
True Clusterings			
Longest DA	0.3655	0.4077	0.3545
Prototype DA	0.3626	0.4140	0.3539
System Clusterings			
using LDA			
Longest DA	0.3623	0.1892	0.2214
Prototype DA	0.3669	0.1887	0.2212
using SVMs			
Longest DA	0.3719	0.1261	0.1682
Prototype DA	0.3816	0.1264	0.1700
No Clustering			
Longest DA	0.1039	0.1382	0.1080
Prototype DA	0.1350	0.1209	0.1138
Upper Bound	0.8970	0.4089	**0.5333**

Table 6: Results for ROUGE-1: Decision Summary Generation Using Unsupervised Methods

Dialogue Act-based Summarization. Previous research (e.g., Murray et al. (2005), Galley (2006), Gurevych and Strube (2004)) has shown that DRDA-level extractive summarization can be effective when viewed as a binary classification task. To implement this approach, we assume that the DRDA to be extracted for the summary is the one with the largest vocabulary overlap with the cluster's gold-standard decision abstract. This DA-level summarization method has an advantage that the summary maintains good readability without a natural language generation component.

Token-based Summarization. As shown in Table 1, some decision-related DAs contain many useless words when compared with the gold-standard abstracts. As a result, we propose a method for token-level decision summarization that focuses on identifying critical keywords from the cluster's DRDAs. We follow the method of Fernández et al. (2008a), but use a larger set of features and different learning methods.

Adding Discourse Context. For each of the supervised DA- and token-based summarization methods, we also investigate the role of the discourse context. Specifically, we augment the DRDA clusterings with additional (not decision-related) DAs from the meeting dialogue: for each decision partition, we include the DA with the highest TF-IDF similarity with the centroid of the partition. We will investigate the possible effects of this additional context on summary quality.

In the next subsection, we describe the features used for supervised learning of DA- and token-based decision summaries.

4.3 Dialogue Cues for Decision Summarization

Different from text, dialogues have some notable features that we expect to be useful for finding informative, decision-related utterances. This section describes some of the dialogue-based features employed in our classifiers. The full lists of features are shown in Table 4 and Table 5.

Structural Information: Adjacency Pairs. An *Adjacency Pair* (AP) is an important conversational analysis concept; APs are considered the fundamental unit of conversational organization (Schegloff and Sacks, 1973). In the AMI corpus, an AP pair consists of a source utterance and a target utterance, produced by different speakers. The source precedes the target but they are not necessarily adjacent. We include features to indicate whether or not two DAs are APs indicating QUESTION+ANSWER or POSITIVE FEEDBACK. For these features, we use the gold-standard AP annotations. We also include one feature that checks membership in a small set of words to decide whether a DA contains positive feedback (e.g., "yeah", "yes").

Discourse Information: Review and Closing Indicator. Another pragmatic cue for dialogue discussion is terms like "wrap up" or "recap", indicating that speakers will review the key meeting content. We include the distance between these indicators and DAs as a feature.

Grammatical Information: Dependency Relation Between Words. For token-level summarization, we make use of the grammatical relationships in the DAs. As in Bui et al. (2009) and Fernández

	CRFs			SVMs		
	PRECISION	RECALL	F1	PRECISION	RECALL	F1
True Clusterings						
DA	0.3922	0.4449	**0.3789**	0.3661	0.4695	0.3727
Token	0.5055	0.2453	0.3033	0.4953	0.3788	**0.3963**
DA+Context	0.3753	0.4372	**0.3678**	0.3595	0.4449	0.3640
Token+Context	0.5682	0.2825	0.3454	0.6213	0.3868	**0.4387**
System Clusterings using LDA						
DA	0.3087	0.1663	**0.1935**	0.3391	0.2097	**0.2349**
Token	0.3379	0.0911	0.1307	0.3760	0.1427	0.1843
DA+Context	0.3305	0.1748	**0.2041**	0.2903	0.1869	**0.2068**
Token+Context	0.4557	0.1198	0.1727	0.4882	0.1486	0.2056
using SVMs						
DA	0.3508	0.1884	**0.2197**	0.3592	0.2026	**0.2348**
Token	0.2807	0.04968	0.0777	0.3607	0.0885	0.1246
DA+Context	0.3583	0.1891	**0.2221**	0.3418	0.1892	**0.2213**
Token+Context	0.4891	0.0822	0.1288	0.4873	0.0914	0.1393
No Clustering						
DA	0.08673	0.1957	0.0993	0.0707	0.1979	0.0916
Token	0.1906	0.0625	0.0868	0.1890	0.3068	0.2057

Table 7: Results for ROUGE-1: Summary Generation Using Supervised Learning

et al. (2008a), we design features that encode (a) basic predicate-argument structures involving major phrase types (S, VP, NP, and PP) and (b) additional typed dependencies from Marneffe et al. (2006). We use the Stanford Parser.

5 Experiments

Experiments based on supervised learning are performed using 3-fold cross-validation. We train two different types of classifiers for identifying informative DAs or tokens: Conditional Random Fields (CRFs) (via Mallet) and Support Vector Machines (SVMs) (via SVM^{light}).

We remove function words from DAs before using them as the input of our systems. The AMI decision abstracts are the gold-standard summaries. We use the ROUGE (Lin and Hovy, 2003) evaluation measure. ROUGE is a recall-based method that can identify systems producing succinct and descriptive summaries.[7]

Results and Analysis. Results for the unsupervised and supervised summarization methods are shown in Tables 6 and 7, respectively. In the tables, TRUE CLUSTERINGS means that we apply our methods on the gold-standard DRDA clusterings. SYSTEM CLUSTERINGS use clusterings obtained from the methods introduced in Section 4; we show results only using the best unsupervised (USING LDA) and supervised (USING SVMS) DRDA clustering techniques.

Both Table 6 and 7 show that some attempt to cluster DRDAs improves the summarization results vs. NO CLUSTERING. In Table 6, there is no significant difference between the results obtained from the LONGEST DA and PROTOTYPE DA for any experiment setting. This is because the longest DA is often selected as the prototype. An UPPER BOUND result is listed for comparison: for each decision cluster, this system selects all words from the DRDAs that are part of the decision abstract (discarding duplicates).

Table 7 presents the results for supervised summarization. Rows starting with DA or TOKEN indicate results at the DA- or token-level. The +CONTEXT rows show results when discourse context is included.[8] We see that: (1) SVMs have a superior or comparable summarization performance vs. CRFs on every task. (2) Token-level summaries perform better than DA-level summaries only using TRUE CLUSTERINGS and the SVM-based summarizer. (3) Discourse context generally improves token-level summaries but not DA-level summaries.[9] (4) DRDA

[7]We use the stemming option of the ROUGE software at http://berouge.com/.

[8]In our experiments, we choose the top 20 relevant DAs as context.

[9]We do not extract words from the discourse context and experiments where we tried this were unsuccessful.

clusterings produced by (unsupervised) LDA lead to summaries that are quite comparable in quality to those generated from DRDA clusterings produced by SVMs (supervised). From Table 6, we see that F1 is 0.2214 when choosing longest DAs from LDA-generated clusterings, which is comparable with the F1s of 0.1935 and 0.2349, attained when employing CRF and SVMs on the same clusterings.

The results in Table 7 are achieved by comparing abstracts having function words with system-generated summaries without function words. To reduce the vocabulary difference as much as possible, we also ran experiments that remove function words from the gold-standard abstracts, but no significant difference is observed.[10]

Finally, we considered comparing our systems to the earlier similar work of (Fernández et al., 2008a) and (Bui et al., 2009), but found that it would be quite difficult because they employ a different notion from DRDAs which is Decision Dialogue Acts(DDAs). In addition, they manually annotate words from their DDAs as the gold-standard summary, guaranteeing that their decision summaries employ the same vocabulary as the DDAs. We instead use the actual decision abstracts from the AMI corpus.

5.1 Sample Decision Summaries

Here we show sample summaries produced using our methods (Table 8). We pick one of the clusterings generated by LDA consisting of four DAs which support two decisions and take SVMs as the supervised summarization method. We remove function words and special markers like "[disfmarker]" from the DAs.

The outputs indicate that either the longest DA or prototype DA contains part of the decisions in this "mixed" cluster. Adding discourse context refines the summaries at both the DA- and token-levels.

DA (1): um of course , as [disfmarker] we , we've already talked about the personal face plates in this meeting , **(a)** **DA (2)**: and I'd like to stick to that . **(a)** **DA (3)**: Well , I guess plastic and coated in rubber . **(b)** **DA (4)**: So the actual remote would be hard plastic and the casings rubber . **(b)**
Decision (a): Will use personal face plates. **Decision (b)**: Case will be plastic and coated in rubber.
Longest DA: talked about personal face plates in meeting **Prototype DA:** actual remote hard plastic casings rubber **DA-level:** talked about personal face plates in meeting, like to stick to, guess plastic and coated in rubber, actual remote hard plastic casings rubber **Token-level:** actual remote plastic casings rubber **DA-level and Discourse Context:** talked about personal face plates in meeting, guess plastic and coated in rubber, actual remote hard plastic casings rubber **Token-level and Discourse Context:** remote plastic rubber

Table 8: Sample system outputs by different methods are in the third cell (methods' names are in bold). First cell contains four DAs. (a) or (b) refers to the decision that DA supports, which is listed in the second cell.

6 Conclusion

In this work, we explore methods for producing decision summaries from spoken meetings at both the DA-level and the token-level. We show that clustering DRDAs before identifying informative content to extract can improve summarization quality. We also find that unsupervised clustering of DRDAs (using LDA-based topic models) can produce summaries of comparable quality to those generated from supervised DRDA clustering. Token-level summarization methods can be boosted by adding discourse context and outperform DA-level summarization when true DRDA clusterings are available; otherwise, DA-level summarization methods offer better performance.

[10]Given abstracts without function words, and using the clusterings generated by LDA and employ CRF on DA- and token-level summarization, we get F1s of 0.1954 and 0.1329, which is marginally better than the corresponding 0.1935 and 0.1307 in Table 7. Similarly, if SVMs are employed in the same cases, we get F1s of 0.2367 and 0.1861 instead of 0.2349 and 0.1843. All of the other results obtain negligible minor increases in F1.

Acknowledgments. This work was supported in part by National Science Foundation Grants IIS-0535099 and IIS-0968450, and by a gift from Google.

References

Amit Bagga and Breck Baldwin. 1998. Algorithms for scoring coreference chains. In *In The First International Conference on Language Resources and Evaluation Workshop on Linguistics Coreference*, pages 563–566.

Satanjeev Banerjee, Carolyn Penstein Rosé, and Alexander I. Rudnicky. 2005. The necessity of a meeting recording and playback system, and the benefit of topic-level annotations to meeting browsing. In *INTERACT*, pages 643–656.

Adam L. Berger, Vincent J. Della Pietra, and Stephen A. Della Pietra. 1996. A maximum entropy approach to natural language processing. *Comput. Linguist.*, 22:39–71, March.

David M. Blei, Andrew Y. Ng, and Michael I. Jordan. 2003. Latent dirichlet allocation. *J. Mach. Learn. Res.*, 3:993–1022, March.

Trung H. Bui, Matthew Frampton, John Dowding, and Stanley Peters. 2009. Extracting decisions from multi-party dialogue using directed graphical models and semantic similarity. In *Proceedings of the SIGDIAL 2009 Conference*, pages 235–243.

Anne Hendrik Buist, Wessel Kraaij, and Stephan Raaijmakers. 2004. Automatic summarization of meeting data: A feasibility study. In *in Proc. Meeting of Computational Linguistics in the Netherlands (CLIN*.

Jean Carletta, Simone Ashby, Sebastien Bourban, Mike Flynn, Thomas Hain, Jaroslav Kadlec, Vasilis Karaiskos, Wessel Kraaij, Melissa Kronenthal, Guillaume Lathoud, Mike Lincoln, Agnes Lisowska, and Mccowan Wilfried Post Dennis Reidsma. 2005. The ami meeting corpus: A pre-announcement. In *In Proc. MLMI*, pages 28–39.

Freddy Y. Y. Choi. 2000. Advances in domain independent linear text segmentation. In *Proceedings of the 1st North American chapter of the Association for Computational Linguistics conference*, pages 26–33.

Raquel Fernández, Matthew Frampton, John Dowding, Anish Adukuzhiyil, Patrick Ehlen, and Stanley Peters. 2008a. Identifying relevant phrases to summarize decisions in spoken meetings. INTERSPEECH-2008, pages 78–81.

Raquel Fernández, Matthew Frampton, Patrick Ehlen, Matthew Purver, and Stanley Peters. 2008b. Modelling and detecting decisions in multi-party dialogue. In *Proceedings of the 9th SIGdial Workshop on Discourse and Dialogue*, pages 156–163.

Matthew Frampton, Jia Huang, Trung Huu Bui, and Stanley Peters. 2009. Real-time decision detection in multi-party dialogue. In *Proceedings of the 2009 Conference on Empirical Methods in Natural Language Processing: Volume 3 - Volume 3*, pages 1133–1141.

Michel Galley. 2006. A skip-chain conditional random field for ranking meeting utterances by importance. In *Proceedings of the 2006 Conference on Empirical Methods in Natural Language Processing*, pages 364–372.

Iryna Gurevych and Michael Strube. 2004. Semantic similarity applied to spoken dialogue summarization. In *Proceedings of the 20th international conference on Computational Linguistics*.

Pei-Yun Hsueh and Johanna D. Moore. 2008. Automatic decision detection in meeting speech. In *Proceedings of the 4th international conference on Machine learning for multimodal interaction*, pages 168–179.

Thorsten Joachims. 1998. Text categorization with Support Vector Machines: Learning with many relevant features. In Claire Nédellec and Céline Rouveirol, editors, *Machine Learning: ECML-98*, volume 1398, chapter 19, pages 137–142. Berlin/Heidelberg.

Chin-Yew Lin and Eduard Hovy. 2003. Automatic evaluation of summaries using n-gram co-occurrence statistics. In *Proceedings of the 2003 Conference of the North American Chapter of the Association for Computational Linguistics on Human Language Technology - Volume 1*, pages 71–78.

Inderjeet Mani. 1999. *Advances in Automatic Text Summarization*. MIT Press, Cambridge, MA, USA.

Daniel Marcu. 2000. *The Theory and Practice of Discourse Parsing and Summarization*. MIT Press, Cambridge, MA, USA.

M. Marneffe, B. Maccartney, and C. Manning. 2006. Generating Typed Dependency Parses from Phrase Structure Parses. In *Proceedings of LREC-06*, pages 449–454.

Marina Meilă. 2007. Comparing clusterings—an information based distance. *J. Multivar. Anal.*, 98:873–895, May.

Gabriel Murray, Steve Renals, and Jean Carletta. 2005. Extractive summarization of meeting recordings. In *in Proceedings of the 9th European Conference on Speech Communication and Technology*, pages 593–596.

Gerard Salton, Amit Singhal, Mandar Mitra, and Chris Buckley. 1997. Automatic text structuring and summarization. *Inf. Process. Manage.*, 33:193–207, March.

E. A. Schegloff and H. Sacks. 1973. Opening up closings. *Semiotica*, 8(4):289–327.

Shasha Xie, Yang Liu, and Hui Lin. 2008. Evaluating the effectiveness of features and sampling in extractive meeting summarization. In *in Proc. of IEEE Spoken Language Technology (SLT*.

Klaus Zechner. 2002. Automatic summarization of open-domain multiparty dialogues in diverse genres. *Comput. Linguist.*, 28:447–485, December.

Who wrote What Where: Analyzing the content of human and automatic summaries

Karolina Owczarzak and **Hoa Trang Dang**
Information Access Division
National Institute of Standards and Technology
Gaithersburg, MD 20899
karolina.owczarzak@nist.gov hoa.dang@nist.gov

Abstract

Abstractive summarization has been a long-standing and long-term goal in automatic summarization, because systems that can generate abstracts demonstrate a deeper understanding of language and the meaning of documents than systems that merely extract sentences from those documents. Genest (2009) showed that summaries from the top automatic summarizers are judged as comparable to manual extractive summaries, and both are judged to be far less responsive than manual abstracts, As the state of the art approaches the limits of extractive summarization, it becomes even more pressing to advance abstractive summarization. However, abstractive summarization has been sidetracked by questions of what qualifies as important information, and how do we find it? The Guided Summarization task introduced at the Text Analysis Conference 2010 attempts to neutralize both of these problems by introducing topic categories and lists of aspects that a responsive summary should address. This design results in more similar human models, giving the automatic summarizers a more focused target to pursue, and also provides detailed diagnostics of summary content, which can can help build better meaning-oriented summarization systems.

1 Introduction

What qualifies as important information and how do we find it? These questions have been leading research in automatic summarization since its beginnings, and we are still nowhere near a definitive answer. Worse, experiments with humans subjects suggest a definitive answer might not even exist. With all their near-perfect language understanding and world knowledge, two human summarizers will still produce two different summaries of the same text, simply because they will disagree on what's important. Fortunately, usually some of this information will overlap. This is represented by the idea behind the Pyramid evaluation framework (Nenkova and Passonneau, 2004; Passonneau et al., 2005), where different levels of the pyramid represent the proportion of concepts ("Summary Content Units", or SCUs) mentioned by 1 to *n* summarizers in summaries of the same text. Usually, there are very few SCUs that are mentioned by all summarizers, a few more that are mentioned by some of them, and the greatest proportion are the SCUs that are mentioned by individual summarizers only.

This variance in what should be a "gold standard" makes research in automatic summarization methods particularly difficult. How can we reach a goal so vague and under-defined? Using term frequency to determine important concepts in a text has proven to be very successful, largely because of its simplicity and universal applicability, but statistical methods can only provide the most basic level of performance. On the other hand, there is no real motivation to use any deeper meaning-oriented text analysis if we are not even certain what information to look for in order to produce a responsive summary.

To address these concerns, the Summarization track at the 2010 Text Analysis Conference[1] (TAC) introduced a new summarization task – Guided Summarization – in which topics are divided into

[1] All datasets available at http://www.nist.gov/tac/

Proceedings of the Workshop on Automatic Summarization for Different Genres, Media, and Languages, pages 25–32,
Portland, Oregon, June 23, 2011.

narrow categories and a list of required aspects is provided for each category. This serves two purposes: first, it creates a more focused target for automatic summarizers, neutralizing human variance and pointing to concrete types of information the reader requires, and second, it provides a detailed diagnostic tool to analyze the content of automatic summaries, which can help build more meaning-oriented systems. This paper shows how these objectives were achieved in TAC 2010, looking at the similarity of human-crafted models, and then using the category and aspect information to look in depth at the differences between human and top automatic summarizers, discovering strengths and weaknesses of automatic systems and areas for improvement.

2 Topic-specific summarization

The idea that different types of stories might require different approaches is not new, although the classification varies from task to task. Topic categories were present in Document Understanding Conference[2] (DUC) 2001, where topics were divided into: single-event, single-subject, biographical, multiple events of same type, and opinion. In their analysis of these results, Nenkova and Louis (2008) find that summaries of articles in what they call *topic-cohesive* categories (single-event, single-subject, biography) are of higher quality than those in *non-cohesive* categories (opinion, multiple event).

In essence, categorizing topics into types is based on the assumption that stories of the same type follow a specific template and include the same kinds of facts, and this predictability might be employed to improve the summarization process, since we at least know *what kinds of information* are important and what to look for. This was shown, among others, by Bagga (1997), who analyzed source articles used in the Message Understanding Conference (MUC) and graphed the distribution of facts in articles on air vehicle launches, terrorist attacks, joint ventures, and corporate personnel changes, finding that the same kinds of facts appeared repeatedly. A natural conclusion is that Information Extraction (IE) methods might be helpful here, and in fact, White et al. (2001) presented an IE-based summarization system for natural disasters, where they first filled an IE template with slots related to date, location, type of disaster, damage (people, physical effects), etc. Similarly, Radev and McKeown (1998) used IE combined with Natural Language Generation (NLG) in their SUMMON system.

There are two ways to classify stories: according to their level of cohesiveness (to use the distinction made by Nenkova and Louis (2008)), and according to subject. The first classification could help us determine which topics would be easier for automatic summarization, but the difficulty is related purely to lexical characteristics of the text; as shown in Louis and Nenkova (2009), source document similarity in terms of word overlap is one of the predictive features of multi-document summary quality. The second classification, according to subject matter, is what enables us to utilize more meaning-oriented approaches such as IE and attempt a deeper semantic analysis of the source text, and is what we describe in this paper.

3 Guided summarization at TAC

The new guided summarization task in 2010 was designed with the second classification in mind, in order to afford the participants a chance to explore deeper linguistic methods of text analysis. There were five topic categories: (1) Accidents and Natural Disasters, (2) Attacks (Criminal/Terrorist), (3) Health and Safety, (4) Endangered Resources, and (5) Trials and Investigations (Criminal/Legal/Other).[3] In contrast to previous topic-specific summarization tasks, the Guided Summarization task also provided a list of required aspects, which described the type of information that should be included in the summary (if such information could be found in source documents). Summarizers also had the option of including any other information they deemed important to the topic. The categories and their aspects, shown in Table 1, were developed on the basis of past DUC and TAC topics and model summaries from years 2001-2009.

Each topic came with 20 chronologically ordered

[2]http://www-nlpir.nist.gov/projects/duc/

[3]In the remainder of this paper, the following short forms are used for names of categories: Accidents = Accidents and Natural Disasters; Attacks = Attacks; Health = Health and Safety; Resources = Endangered Resources; Trials = Trials and Investigations. Full description of the task is available at the TAC website.

Accidents	Attacks	Health
what	what	what
when	when	who affected
where	where	how
why	perpertrators	why
who affected	why	countermeasures
damages	who affected	
countermeasures	damages	
	countermeasures	

Resources	Trials
what	who
importance	who investigating
threats	why
countermeasures	charges
	plead
	sentence

Table 1: Categories and aspects in TAC 2010 Guided Summarization task.

		human		automatic	
		initial	update	initial	update
Pyramid	2008	0.66	0.63	0.26	0.20
	2009	0.68	0.60	0.26	0.20
	2010	0.78	0.67	0.30	0.20
Respons.	2008	4.62	4.62	2.32	2.02
	2009	4.66	4.48	2.32	2.17
	2010	4.76	4.71	2.56	2.10

Table 2: Macro-average Pyramid and Responsiveness scores for initial and update summaries for years 2008-2010. Responsiveness scores for 2009 were scaled from a ten-point to a five-point scale.

news articles. The *initial* summaries were to be produced on the basis of the first 10 documents. As in TAC 2008 and 2009, the 2010 Summarization task had an update component: using the second 10 documents, summarizers were to produce an *update* summary under the assumption that the user had already read the first set of source documents. This means that for the update part, there were two interacting conditions, with the requirement for non-redundancy taking priority over the requirement to address all category aspects.

For each topic, four model summaries were written by human assessors. All summaries were evaluated with respect to linguistic quality (Overall Readability), content (Pyramid), and general quality (Overall Responsiveness). Readability and Responsiveness were judged by human assessors on a scale from 1 (very poor) to 5 (very good), while Pyramid is a score between 0 and 1 (in very rare cases, it exceeds 1, if the candidate summary contains more SCUs than the *average* reference summary).

Since this was the first year of Guided Summarization, only about half of the 43 participating systems made some use of the provided categories and aspects, mostly using them and their synonyms as query terms.

3.1 Model summaries across years

The introduction of categories, which implies template story types, and aspects, which further narrows content selection, resulted in the parallel model summaries being much more similar to each other than in previous years, as represented by the Pyramid score, which measures information overlap between a candidate summary and a set of reference summaries. Table 2 shows the macro-averaged Pyramid and Responsiveness scores for years 2008-2010. Both initial and update human summaries score higher for Pyramid in 2010, and also gain a little in Responsiveness. The macro-averages for automatic summarizers, on the other hand, increase only for initial summaries, which we will discuss further in Section 3.4. The similarity effect among model summaries can be more clearly seen in Table 3, which shows the percentage of Summary Content Units (SCUs, information "nuggets"or simple facts) with different weights in Pyramids across the years between 2008-2010. The weight of an SCU is simply the number of model summaries in which this information unit appears. Pyramids in 2010 have greater percentage of SCUs with weight > 1, and their proportion of weight-1 SCUs is below half of all SCUs. The difference is much more pronounced for the initial summaries, since the update component is restricted by the non-redundancy requirement, resulting in more variance in content selection after the required aspects have been covered.[4]

3.2 Content coverage in TAC 2010

During the Pyramid creation process, assessors extracting SCUs from model summaries were asked to mark the aspect(s) relevant to each SCU. This lets us examine and compare the distribution of information in human and automatic summaries. Table 4 shows macro-average SCU counts in Pyramids com-

[4]Each summary could be up to 100 words long, and no incentive was given for writing summaries of shorter length; therefore, the goal for both human and automatic summarizers was to fit as much relevant information as possible in the 100-word limit.

	SCU weight	2008	2009	2010
initial	4	9%	12%	22%
	3	14%	13%	18%
	2	22%	23%	24%
	1	55%	52%	36%
update	4	8%	7%	11%
	3	12%	12%	14%
	2	21%	20%	26%
	1	59%	62%	49%

Table 3: Percentage of SCUs with weights 1–4 in pyramids for initial and update summaries for years 2008-2010.

	SCU weight	initial		update	
		pyramids	automatic	pyramids	automatic
Accidents	4	6.4	3.2	1.9	0.5
	3	3.7	1	3.43	0.8
	2	6.9	1.6	6.1	0.6
	1	7.9	0.8	7.6	0.7
	total	24.9	7.7	19.1	3.1
Attacks	4	7.7	4.9	3.7	1
	3	3.1	0.8	3.7	0.8
	2	5	1	5.3	0.8
	1	5.6	0.5	9.4	0.7
	total	21.4	9.1	22.1	3.9
Health	4	4.9	1.8	1.6	0.4
	3	4.2	0.8	2.6	0.7
	2	5.3	0.6	4.9	0.8
	1	10.6	0.9	12	0.8
	total	25	5	21	3
Resources	4	4.2	1.5	1.1	0.6
	3	5.1	1.3	2.7	0.5
	2	5	1	5.9	1
	1	9.5	0.7	12.4	1
	total	23.8	5	22.1	3.4
Trials	4	4.4	2.6	3.4	1.2
	3	5.7	2	3.3	0.5
	2	7.8	1.6	5.7	0.6
	1	9.2	0.5	8.5	0.6
	total	27.1	8.5	20.9	3.3

Table 4: Macro-average SCU counts with weights 1–4 in pyramids and matching SCU counts in automatic summaries, for initial and update summaries.

posed of four human summaries, and macro-average counts of matching SCUs in the summaries of the 15 top-performing automatic summarizers (as determined by their Responsiveness rank on initial summaries).[5] Although automatic summaries find only a small percentage of all available information (as represented by the number of Pyramid SCUs), the SCUs they find for the initial summaries are usually those of the highest weight, i.e. encoding information that is the most essential to the topic.

SCU distribution in human summaries is also interesting: Health, Resources, and Trials all have the expected pyramid shape, with many low-weight SCUs at the base and few high-weight SCUs on top, but for Attacks and Accidents, the usual pattern is broken and we see an hourglass shape instead, reflecting the presence of many weight-4 SCUs. The most likely explanation is that these two categories are guided by a relatively long list of aspects (cf. Table 1), many of which have unique answers in the source text.

This is shown in more detail in Table 5, which presents aspect coverage by Pyramids and top 15 automatic summarizers in terms of an average number of SCUs relevant to a given aspect and an average weight of an aspect-related SCU. Only Attack and Accidents have aspects that tend to generate the same answers from almost all human summarizers: *when*, *where* in Accidents and *what*, *when*, *where*, *perpetrators*, and *who_affected* in Attacks all have average weight of around 3. The patterns hold for update summaries; although all values decrease and there is less overlap between models, answers to these aspects are the most likely to occur in multiple summaries.

The situation for top 15 automatic summarizers is even more interesting: while they contain relatively few matching SCUs, the SCUs they do find are those of high weight, as can be seen by comparing their SCU weight averages. Even for "other", which covers "all other information important for the topic" and is therefore more dependent on summary writer's subjective judgment and shows more content diversity, resulting in low-weight SCUs in the Pyramid, the top automatic summarizers find those most weighted. It would seem, then, that the content selection methods are able to identify some of the most important facts; at the same time, the density of information in automatic summaries is much lower than in human summaries, indicating that the automatic content is either not compressed adequately, or that it includes non-relevant or repeated information.

[5] We chose to use the top 15 out of 43 participating systems in order to exclude outliers like systems that returned empty summaries, and to measure the state-of-the-art in the summarization field.

		Avg SCU weight (avg SCU count)			
		initial summaries		update summaries	
		Pyramids	automatic	Pyramids	automatic
Accidents	what	2.4 (4.4)	3.1 (1.9)	2.5 (2.7)	2.87 (0.6)
	when	3.6 (2.1)	3.7 (0.7)	3.7 (0.4)	4 (0.1)
	where	3.0 (3.6)	3.2 (1.3)	2.1 (1.1)	2.58 (0.4)
	why	2.6 (2.3)	3.1 (0.5)	2.4 (2.0)	3 (0.3)
	who_aff	2.3 (4.9)	2.8 (1.5)	2.0 (4.1)	2.45 (0.6)
	damages	1.8 (2.4)	3.1 (0.5)	1.7 (1.9)	2.05 (0.2)
	counterm	2.1 (8.0)	2.7 (1.2)	2.0 (8.1)	2.4 (0.9)
	other	1.3 (0.4)	1.9 (0.1)	1.3 (0.6)	1 (0.0)
Attacks	what	2.9 (3.1)	3.7 (1.6)	2.0 (1.4)	2.8 (0.4)
	when	3.4 (1.3)	3.8 (0.4)	2.4 (1.4)	2.2 (0.1)
	where	2.7 (2.9)	3.7 (1.2)	2.5 (0.9)	3.8 (0.3)
	perpetr	2.8 (3.6)	3.4 (1.0)	2.2 (3.0)	3.0 (0.9)
	why	2.1 (3.4)	2.8 (0.9)	1.8 (1.3)	1.6 (0.2)
	who_aff	3.3 (4.0)	3.6 (1.7)	2.0 (2.0)	2.1 (0.3)
	damages	2.2 (0.9)	3.0 (0.2)	3.4 (0.7)	4.0 (0.1)
	counterm	2.3 (4.3)	2.8 (1.1)	2.1 (10.3)	2.6 (1.1)
	other	1.7 (1.3)	2.2 (0.1)	1.6 (2.6)	1.7 (0.2)
Health	what	2.4 (6.0)	3.1 (1.6)	2.4 (2.9)	3.0 (0.7)
	who_aff	2.0 (5.6)	2.6 (0.8)	1.8 (2.7)	2.0 (0.3)
	how	2.4 (6.6)	3.1 (1.1)	1.6 (2.7)	2.4 (0.3)
	why	2.2 (3.9)	2.9 (0.6)	1.7 (2.3)	2.1 (0.4)
	counterm	2.0 (6.3)	2.7 (0.8)	1.7 (10.4)	2.2 (1.0)
	other	1.1 (0.6)	1.9 (0.1)	1.2 (1.9)	1.6 (0.2)
Resources	what	2.3 (3.2)	2.9 (1.3)	1.6 (1.4)	2.6 (0.4)
	importan	2.4 (3.1)	2.7 (0.3)	1.8 (1.9)	2.3 (0.2)
	threats	2.3 (7.6)	2.8 (1.6)	1.6 (6.8)	2.0 (1.1)
	counterm	2.0 (10.1)	2.8 (1.7)	1.7 (12.1)	2.2 (1.4)
	other	1.4 (0.7)	2.9 (0.1)	1.8 (1.2)	2.5 (0.1)
Trials	who	2.7 (3.5)	3.2 (1.7)	2.7 (2.3)	3.2 (0.4)
	who_inv	1.9 (5.5)	2.8 (0.8)	1.8 (3.3)	2.6 (0.5)
	why	2.6 (6.3)	3.1 (2.2)	1.8 (2.4)	2.3 (0.3)
	charges	2.7 (2.4)	3.2 (0.8)	2.4 (1.4)	2.5 (0.3)
	plead	2.0 (5.0)	2.9 (0.9)	2.1 (3.5)	3.0 (0.5)
	sentence	2.3 (2.7)	3.0 (0.5)	2.6 (6.0)	3.5 (0.8)
	other	1.5 (3.2)	2.0 (0.3)	1.7 (4.8)	2.4 (0.6)

Table 5: Aspect coverage for Pyramids and top 15 automatic summarizers in TAC 2010.

3.3 Effect of categories and aspects

Some categories in the Guided Summarization task are defined in more detail than others, depending on types of stories they represent. Stories about attacks and accidents (and, to some extent, trials) tend to follow more predictable and detailed templates, which results in more similar models and better results for automatic summarizers. Figure 1 gives a graphic representation of the macro-average Pyramid and Responsiveness scores for human and top 15 automatic summarizers, with exact scores in Tables 6 and 7, where the first score marked with a letter is not statistically significant from any subsequent score marked with the same letter, according to ANOVA ($p>0.05$). Lack of significant difference between human Responsiveness scores in Table 6 suggests that, for all categories, human summaries are highly and equally responsive, but a look at their Pyramid scores confirms that Attacks and Accidents models tend to have more overlapping information.

For automatic summaries, their Pyramid and Responsiveness patterns are parallel. Here Attacks, Accidents, and Trials contain on average more matching SCUs than Health and Resources, making these summaries more responsive. One reason for these differences might be that many systems rely on sentence positon in the extraction process, and first sentences in these template stories often are a short description of event including date, location, persons involved, in effect giving systems the unique-answer aspects mentioned in Section 3.2. Table 5 shows this distribution of matching information in more detail: for Attacks and Accidents, automatic summarizers match relatively more SCUs for *what*, *where*, *when*, *who_affected* than for *countermeasures*, *damages*, or *other*. For Trials, again the easier aspects are those that tend to appear at the beginning of documents: *who* [is under investigation] and *why*. Stories in Health and Resources, the weakest categories overall for automatic summarizers and with the greatest amount of variance for human summarizers, are non-events, instead being closer to what in past DUC tasks was described as a "multi-event" or "single subject" story type. Individual documents within the source set might sometimes follow the typical event template (e.g. describing individual instances of coral reef destruction), but in general these categories require much more abstraction and render the opening-sentence extraction strategy less effective.

If the higher averages are really due to the information extracted with first sentences, then we would also expect higher scores from Baseline 1, which simply selected the opening sentences of the most recent document, up to the 100-word limit. And indeed, as shown in Table 8, the partial Pyramid scores for Baseline 1 are the highest for exactly these "concrete" categories and aspects, mostly for Attacks and Accidents, and aspects such as *where*, *what*, and *who* (the score of 1 for Accidents *other* is an outlier, since there was only one SCU relevant for this calculation and the baseline happened to match it). On the other hand, its lowest performance is mostly concentrated in Health and Resources, and in the more "vague" aspects, like *why*, *how*, *importance*, *coun-*

	Pyramid		Responsiveness	
initial	Attacks	0.857 *A*	Trials	4.825 *A*
	Accidents	0.812 *AB*	Accidents	4.821 *AB*
	Resources	0.773 *AB*	Attacks	4.786 *ABC*
	Health	0.767 *AB*	Health	4.750 *ABCD*
	Trials	0.751 *B*	Resources	4.650 *ABCD*
update	Trials	0.749 *A*	Attack	4.857 *A*
	Attacks	0.745 *AB*	Trials	4.825 *AB*
	Accidents	0.700 *AB*	Accidents	4.714 *ABC*
	Health	0.610 *C*	Health	4.625 *ABCD*
	Resources	0.604 *C*	Resources	4.600 *ABCD*

Table 6: Macro-average Pyramid and Responsiveness scores per category for human summaries, comparison across categories.

	Pyramid		Responsiveness	
initial	Attacks	0.524 *A*	Attacks	3.400 *A*
	Trials	0.446 *B*	Accidents	3.362 *AB*
	Accidents	0.418 *B*	Trials	3.167 *ABC*
	Resources	0.323 *C*	Resources	2.893 *CD*
	Health	0.290 *C*	Health	2.617 *D*
update	Resources	0.286 *A*	Resources	2.520 *A*
	Trials	0.261 *AB*	Health	2.417 *AB*
	Attacks	0.251 *ABC*	Trials	2.380 *ABC*
	Health	0.236 *BCD*	Attacks	2.286 *ABCD*
	Accidents	0.228 *BCD*	Accidents	2.248 *ABCD*

Table 7: Macro-average Pyramid and Responsiveness scores per category for top 15 automatic summaries, comparison across categories.

termeasures, and *other*. We can conclude that early sentence position is not a good predictor of such information, and that automatic summarizers might do well to diversify their methods of content identification based on what type of information they are looking for.

3.4 Initial and update summaries

While the initial component is only guided by the categories and aspects, the update component is placed under an overarching condition of non-redundancy. Update summaries should not repeat

Highest			Lowest		
Category	Aspect	score	Category	Aspect	score
(Accidents	Other	1)	Resources	other	0
Attacks	WHERE	0.66	Health	other	0
Attacks	WHAT	0.66	Attacks	COUNTERM	0
Trials	WHO	0.6	Attacks	other	0
Attacks	WHO_AFF	0.56	Accidents	WHY	0
Accidents	WHERE	0.44	Health	WHO_AFF	0
Accidents	WHAT	0.41	Trials	SENTENCE	0.06
Trials	WHY	0.38	Health	WHY	0.06
Attacks	PERP	0.34	Accidents	DAMAGES	0.07
Trials	WHO_INV	0.33	Health	HOW	0.08
Trials	CHARGES	0.33	Resources	IMPORTAN	0.09

Table 8: Top Pyramid scores for Baseline 1, per aspect, for initial summaries.

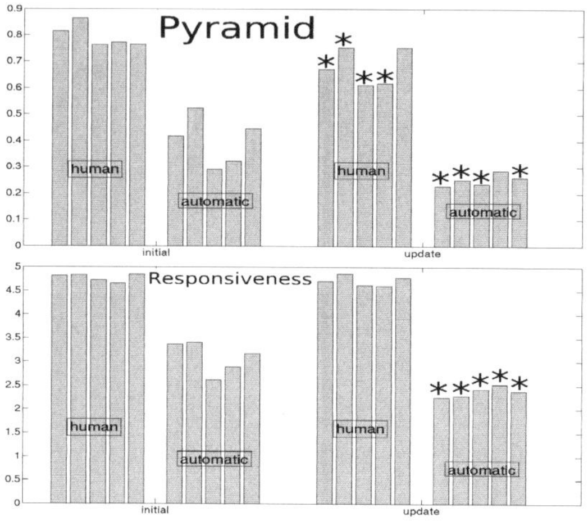

Figure 1: Macro-average Pyramid and Responsiveness scores in initial and update summaries, for humans and top 15 automatic systems. In each group, columns from left: Accidents, Attacks, Health, Resources, Trials. Asterisk indicates significant drop from initial score.

any information that can be found in the initial document set. This restriction narrows the pool of potential summary elements to choose from. More importantly, since the concrete aspects with unique answers like *what*, *where*, and *when* are likely to be mentioned in the first set of document (and, by extension, in the initial summaries), this shifts content selection to aspects that generate more variance, like *why*, *countermeasures*, or *other*. As shown in Figure 1, while Responsiveness remains high for human summarizers across categories, which means the content is still relevant to the topic, the Pyramid scores are lower in the update component, which means the summarizers differ more in terms of what information they extract from the source documents. Note that this is not the case for Trials, where the human performance for both Responsiveness and Pyramid is practically identical for initial and update summaries. The time course of trials is generally longer than those for accidents and attacks, and many of the later-occurring aspects such as plea and sentence are well-defined; hence the initial and update human summaries have similar Pyramid scores. Automatic summarizers, on the other hand, suffer the greatest drop in those categories in which they were the most successful before: Attacks, Accidents, and Trials, in effect rendering their performance across categories more or less even (cf. Figure 1).

A closer look at the aspect coverage in initial and update components confirms the differences in aspect distribution. Figure 2 gives four columns for each aspect: the first two columns represent initial summaries, the second two represent update summaries. Dark columns in each pair are human summarizers, light columns are top 15 automatic summarizers. For almost all aspects, humans find fewer relevant (and new!) facts in the update documents, with the exception of *sentence* in Trials, and *countermeasures* and *other* in all categories. Logically, once all the anchoring information has been given (date, time, location, event), the only remaining relevant content to focus on are consequences of the event (*countermeasures*, *sentence*), and possibly updates in victims and damages (*who_affected*, *damages*) as well as any *other* information that might be relevant. A similar (though less consistent) pattern holds for automatic summarizers.

4 Summary and conclusions

Initial attempts at more complex treatments of any subject often fail when faced with unrestricted, "real world" input. This is why almost all research in summarization remains centered around relatively simple extractive methods. Few developers try to incorporate syntactic parsing to compress summary sentences, and almost none want to venture into semantic decompositon of source text, since the complexity of these methods is the cause of potential errors. Also, the tools might not deal particularly well with different types of stories in the "newswire" genre. However, Genest (2009) showed the limits of purely extractive summarization: their manual, extractive summarizer (HexTac) performed much worse than human abstractors, and comparably to the top automatic summarizers in TAC 2009.

But if we want to see significant progress in abstractive summarization, it's important to provide a more controlled environment for such experiments. TAC 2010 results show that, first of all, by guiding summary creation we end up with more similar human abstracts than in previous tasks (partly due to the choice of template-like categories, and partly due to the further guiding role of aspects). Narrowing down possible summary content, while exclud-

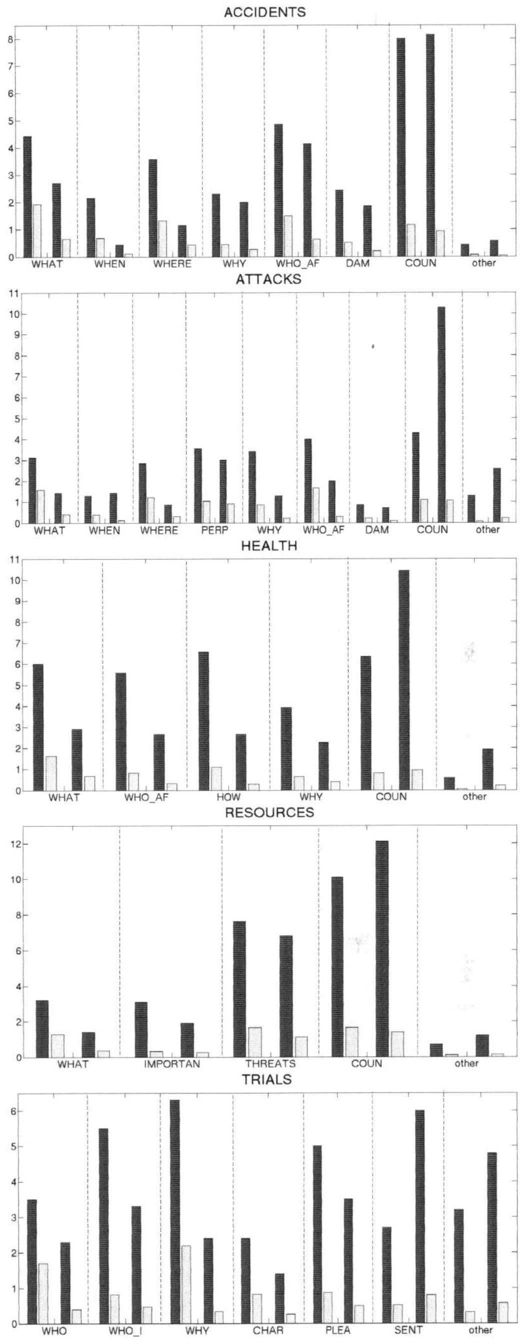

Figure 2: Average number of SCUs per aspect in initial and update summaries in TAC 2010. Dark grey = Pyramids, light grey = top 15 automatic summarizers. The first pair of columns for each aspects shows initial summaries, the second pair shows update summaries.

ing variance due to subjective opinions among human writers, creates in effect a more concrete information model, and a single, unified information model is an easier goal to emulate than relying on vague and subjective goals like "importance". Out of five categories, Attacks and Accidents generated the most similar models, mostly because they required concrete, unique-answer aspects like *where* or *when*. In Health and Resources, the aspects were more subjective in nature, and the resulting variance was greater.

Moreover, the Guided Task provides a very valuable and detailed diagnostic tool for system developers: by looking at the system performance within each aspect, we can find out which types of information it is better able to identify. While the top automatic summarizers managed to retrieve less than half of relevant information at the best of times, the facts they did retrieve were highly-weighted. Their better performance for certain aspects of Attacks, Accidents, and Trials could be ascribed to the fact that most of them rely on sentence position to determine important information in the source document. A comparison of covered aspects suggests that sentence position might be a better indicator for some types of information than others.

Since it was the first year of the Guided Task, only some of the teams used the provided category/aspect information; as the task continues, we hope to see more participants adopting categories and aspects to guide their summarization. The predictable elements of each category invite the use of different techniques depending on the type of information sought, perhaps suggesting the use of Information Extraction methods. Some categories might be easier to process than others, but even if the information-mining approach cannot be extended to all types of stories, at worst we will end up with better summarization for event-type stories, like attacks, accidents, or trials, which together comprise a large part of reported news.

References

Amit Bagga and Alan W. Biermann. 1997. Analyzing the Complexity of a Domain With Respect To An Information Extraction Task. *Proceedings of the tenth International Conference on Research on Computational Linguistics (ROCLING X)*, 175–194.

Pierre-Etienne Genest, Guy Lapalme, and Mehdi Yousfi-Monod. 2009. HEXTAC: the Creation of a Manual Extractive Run. *Proceedings of the Text Analysis Conference 2009*.

Annie Louis and Ani Nenkova. 2009. Performance confidence estimation for automatic summarization. *Proceedings of the 12th Conference of the European Chapter of the Association for Computational Linguistics*, 541–548. Athens, Greece.

Kathleen R. McKeown, Regina Barzilay, David Evans, Vasileios Hatzivassiloglou, Judith L. Klavans, Ani Nenkova, Carl Sable, Barry Schiffman, and Sergey Sigelman. 2002. Tracking and summarizing news on a daily basis with Columbia's Newsblaster. *Proceedings of the Second International Conference on Human Language Technology Research*, 280–285. San Diego, California.

Ani Nenkova and Annie Louis. 2008. Can You Summarize This? Identifying Correlates of Input Difficulty for Multi-Document Summarization. *Proceedings of ACL-08: HLT*, 825–833. Columbus, Ohio.

Ani Nenkova and Rebecca J. Passonneau. 2004. Evaluating content selection in summarization: The Pyramid method. *Proceedings of the Human Language Technology Conference of the North American Chapter of the Association for Computational Linguistics*, 145–152. Boston, MA.

Rebecca J. Passonneau, Ani Nenkova, Kathleen McKeown, and Sergey Sigelman. 2005. Applying the Pyramid method in DUC 2005. *Proceedings of the 5th Document Understanding Conference (DUC)*. Vancouver, Canada.

Dragomir R. Radev and Kathleen R. McKeown. 1998. Generating natural language summaries from multiple on-line sources. *Computational Linguistics*, 24(3):470–500.

Michael White, Tanya Korelsky, Claire Cardie, Vincent Ng, David Pierce, and Kiri Wagstaff. Multidocument summarization via information extraction. 2001. *Proceedings of the First International Conference on Human Language Technology Research*, 1–7. San Diego, California.

WikiTopics: What is Popular on Wikipedia and Why

Byung Gyu Ahn[1] and **Benjamin Van Durme**[1,2] and **Chris Callison-Burch**[1]
[1]Center for Language and Speech Processing
[2]Human Language Technology Center of Excellence
Johns Hopkins University

Abstract

We establish a novel task in the spirit of news summarization and topic detection and tracking (TDT): daily determination of the topics newly popular with Wikipedia readers. Central to this effort is a new public dataset consisting of the hourly page view statistics of all Wikipedia articles over the last three years. We give baseline results for the tasks of: discovering individual pages of interest, clustering these pages into coherent topics, and extracting the most relevant summarizing sentence for the reader. When compared to human judgements, our system shows the viability of this task, and opens the door to a range of exciting future work.

1 Introduction

In this paper we analyze a novel dataset: we have collected the hourly page view statistics[1] for every Wikipedia page in every language for the last three years. We show how these page view statistics, along with other features like article text and inter-page hyperlinks, can be used to identify and explain popular trends, including popular films and music, sports championships, elections, natural disasters, etc.

Our approach is to select a set of articles whose daily pageviews for the last fifteen days dramatically increase above those of the preceding fifteen day period. Rather than simply selecting the most popular articles for a given day, this selects articles whose popularity is rapidly increasing. These popularity spikes tend to be due to significant current events in the real world. We examine 100 such articles for each of 5 randomly selected days in 2009 and attempt to group the articles into clusters such that the clusters coherently correspond to current events and extract a summarizing sentence that best explains the relevant event. Quantitative and qualitative analyses are provided along with the evaluation dataset.

[1]The data does not contain any identifying information about who viewed the pages. See http://dammit.lt/wikistats

Barack Obama
Joe Biden
White House
Inauguration
...
US Airways Flight 1549
Chesley Sullenberger
Hudson River
...
Super Bowl
Arizona Cardinals

Figure 1: Automatically selected articles for Jan 27, 2009.

We compare our automatically collected articles to those in the daily current events portal of Wikipedia where Wikipedia editors manually chronicle current events, which comprise armed conflicts, international relations, law and crime, natural disasters, social, political, sports events, etc. Each event is summarized with a simple phrase or sentence that links to related articles. We view our work as an automatic mechanism that could potentially supplant this hand-curated method of selecting current events by editors.

Figure 1 shows examples of automatically selected articles for January 27, 2009. We would group the articles into 3 clusters, {*Barack Obama*, *Joe Biden*, *White House*, *Inauguration*} which corresponds to the inauguration of Barack Obama, {*US Airways Flight 1549*, *Chesley Sullenburger*, *Hudson River*} which corresponds to the successful ditching of an airplane into the Hudson river without loss of life, and {*Superbowl*, *Arizona Cardinals*} which corresponds to the then upcoming Superbowl XLIII.

We further try to explain the clusters by selecting sentences from the articles. For the first cluster, a good selection would be “the inauguration of Barack Obama as the 44th president ... took place on January 20, 2009”. For the second cluster, “Chesley Burnett ‘Sully’ Sullenberger III (born January 23, 1951) is an American com-

Proceedings of the Workshop on Automatic Summarization for Different Genres, Media, and Languages, pages 33–40,
Portland, Oregon, June 23, 2011.

mercial airline pilot, . . . , who successfully carried out the emergency water landing of US Airways Flight 1549 on the Hudson River, offshore from Manhattan, New York City, on January 15, 2009, . . . " would be a nice summary, which also provides links to the other articles in the same cluster. For the third cluster, "Superbowl XLIII will feature the American Football Conference champion Pittsburgh Steelers (14-4) and the National Football Conference champion Arizona Cardinals (12-7) ." would be a good choice which delineates the association with *Arizona Cardinals*.

Different clustering methods and sentence selection features are evaluated and results are compared. Topic models, such as K-means (Manning et al., 2008) vector space clustering and latent Dirichlet allocation (Blei et al., 2003), are compared to clustering using Wikipedia's link structure. To select sentences we make use of NLP technologies such as coreference resolution, and named entity and date taggers. Note that the latest revision of each article on the day on which the article is selected is used in clustering and textualization to simulate the situation where article selection, clustering, and textualization are performed once every day.

Figure 2 illustrates the pipeline of our WikiTopics system: article selection, clustering, and textualization.

2 Article selection

We would like to identify an uptrend in popularity of articles. In an online encyclopedia such as Wikipedia, the pageviews for an article reflect its popularity. Following the Trending Topics software[2], WikiTopics's articles selection algorithm determines each articles' monthly trend value as increase in pageviews within last 30 days. The monthly trend value t^k of an article k is defined as below:

$$t^k = \sum_{i=1}^{15} d_i^k - \sum_{i=16}^{30} d_i^k$$

where

$$d_i^k = \text{daily pageviews } i-1 \text{ days ago for an article } k$$

We selected 100 articles of the highest trend value for each day in 2009. We call the articles WikiTopics articles. We leave as future work other possibilities to determine the trend value and choose articles[3], and only briefly discuss some alternatives in this section.

Wikipedia has a portal page called "current events", in which significant current events are listed manually by Wikipedia editors. Figure 3 illustrates spikes in

[2]http://www.trendingtopics.org

[3]For example, one might leverage additional signals of real world events, such as Twitter feeds, etc.

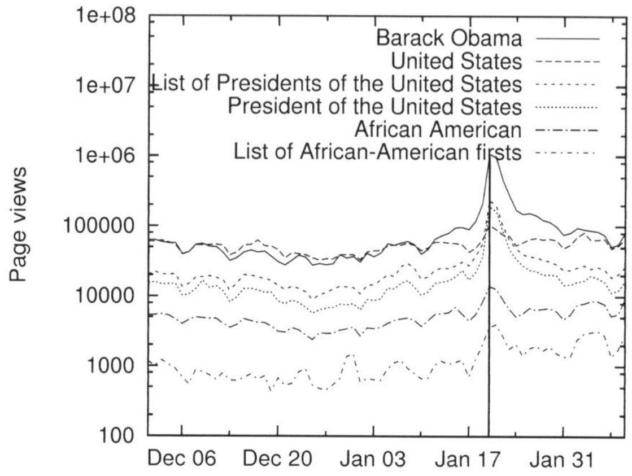

Figure 3: Pageviews for all the hand-curated articles related to the inauguration of Barack Obama. Pageviews spike on the same day as the event took place–January 20, 2009.

pageviews of the hand-curated articles related to the inauguration of Barack Obama, which shows clear correlation between the spikes and the day on which the relevant event took place. It is natural to contrast WikiTopics articles to this set of hand-curated articles. We evaluated WikiTopics articles against hand-curated articles as gold standard and had negative results with precision of 0.13 and recall of 0.28.

There are a few reasons for this. First, there are much fewer hand-curated articles than WikiTopics articles: 17,253 hand-selected articles vs 36,400[4] WikiTopics articles; so precision cannot be higher than 47%. Second, many of the hand-selected articles turned out to have very low pageviews: 6,294 articles (36.5%) have maximum daily pageviews less than 1,000 whereas WikiTopics articles have increase in pageviews of at least 10,000. It is extremely hard to predict the hand-curated articles based on pageviews. Figure 4 further illustrates hand-curated articles' lack of increase in pageviews as opposed to WikiTopics articles. On the contrary, nearly half of the hand-curated articles have decrease in pageviews. For the hand-curated articles, it seems that spikes in pageviews are an exception rather than a commonality. We therefore concluded that it is futile to predict hand-curated articles based on pageviews. The hand-curated articles suffer from low popularity and do not spike in pageviews often. Figure 5 contrasts the WikiTopics articles and the hand-curated articles. The WikiTopics articles shown here do not appear in the hand-curated articles within fifteen days before or after, and vice versa. WikiTopics selected articles about people who played a minor role in the relevant event, recently released films, their protagonists, popular TV series, etc. Wikipedia editors selected articles about

[4]One day is missing from our 2009 pageviews statistics.

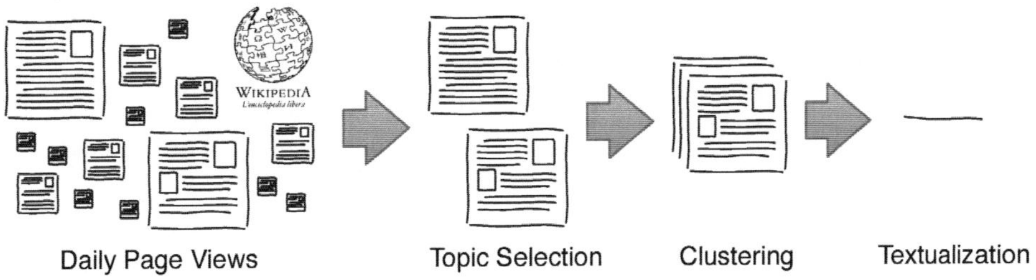

Figure 2: Process diagram: (a) Topic selection: select interesting articles based on increase in pageviews. (b) Clustering: cluster the articles according to relevant events using topic models or Wikipedia's hyperlink structure. (c) Textualization: select the sentence that best summarizes the relevant event.

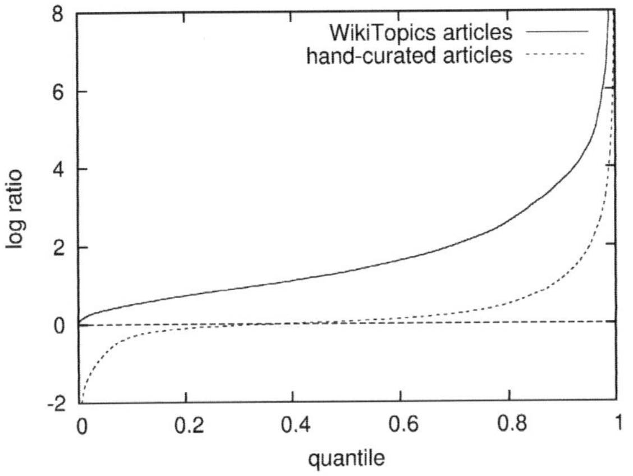

Figure 4: Log ratio of the increase in pageviews: $\log \sum i = 1^{15} di^k / \sum i = 16^{30}$. Zero means no change in pageviews. WikiTopics articles show pageviews increase in a few orders of magnitude as opposed to hand-curated articles.

WikiTopics articles
Joe Biden
Notorious (2009 film)
The Notorious B.I.G.
Lost (TV series)
...
hand-curated articles
Fraud
Florida
Hedge fund
Arthur Nadel
Federal Bureau of Investigation

Figure 5: Illustrative articles for January 27, 2009. WikiTopics articles here do not appear in hand-curated articles within fifteen days before or after, and vice versa. The hand-curated articles shown here are all linked from a single event "Florida hedge fund manager Arthur Nadel is arrested by the United States Federal Bureau of Investigation and charged with fraud."

actions, things, geopolitical or organizational names in the relevant event and their event description mentions all of them.

For this paper we introduce the problem of topic selection along with a baseline solution. There are various viable alternatives to the monthly trend value. As one of them, we did some preliminary experiments with the daily trend value, which is defined by $d_1^k - d_2^k$, i.e. the difference of the pageviews between the day and the previous day: we found that articles selected using the daily trend value have little overlap–less than half the articles overlapped with the monthly trend value. Future work will consider the addition of sources other than pageviews, such as edit histories and Wikipedia category information, along with more intelligent techniques to combine these different sources.

3 Clustering

Clustering plays a central role to identify current events; a group of coherently related articles corresponds to a current event. Clusters, in general, may have hierarchies and an element may be a member of multiple clusters. Whereas Wikipedia's current events are hierarchically compiled into different levels of events, we focus on flat clustering, leaving hierarchical clustering as future work, but allow multiple memberships.

In addition to clustering using Wikipedia's inter-page hyperlink structure, we experimented with two families of clustering algorithms pertaining to topic models: the K-means clustering vector space model and the latent Dirichlet allocation (LDA) probabilistic topic model. We used the Mallet software (McCallum, 2002) to run these topic models. We retrieve the latest revision of each article on the day that WikiTopics selected it. We strip unnecessary HTML tags and Wiki templates with mwlib[5] and split sentences with NLTK (Loper and Bird, 2002). Normalization, tokenization, and stop words removal were performed, but no stemming was performed. The unigram (bag-of-words) model was used and the number

[5]http://code.pediapress.com/wiki/wiki/mwlib

Test set	# Clusters	B^3 F-score
Human-1	48.6	0.70 ± 0.08
Human-2	50.0	0.71 ± 0.11
Human-3	53.8	$\mathbf{0.74 \pm 0.10}$
ConComp	31.8	0.42 ± 0.18
OneHop	45.2	0.58 ± 0.17
K-means tf	50	0.52 ± 0.04
K-means tf-idf	50	$\mathbf{0.58 \pm 0.09}$
LDA	44.8	0.43 ± 0.08

Table 1: Clustering evaluation: F-scores are averaged across gold standard datasets. ConComp and OneHop are using the link structure. K-means clustering with tf-idf performs best. Manual clusters were evaluated against those of the other two annotators to determine inter-annotator agreement.

of clusters/topics K was set to 50, which is the average number of clusters in the human clusters[6]. For K-means, the common settings were used: tf and tf-idf weighting and cosine similarity (Allan et al., 2000). For LDA, we chose the most probable topic for each article as the cluster ID. Two different clustering schemes make use of the inter-page hyperlink structure: ConComp and OneHop. In these schemes, the link structure is treated as a graph, in which each page corresponds to a vertex and each link to an undirected edge. ConComp groups a set of articles that are connected together. OneHop chooses an article and groups a set of articles that are directly linked. The number of resulting clusters depends on the order in which you choose an article. To find the minimum or maximum number of such clusters would be computationally expensive. Instead of attempting to find the optimal number of clusters, we take a greedy approach and iteratively create clusters that maximize the central node connectivity, stopping when all nodes are in at least one cluster. This allows for singleton clusters.

Three annotators manually clustered WikiTopics articles for five randomly selected days. The three manual clusters were evaluated against each other to measure inter-annotator agreement, using the multiplicity B^3 metric (Amigó et al., 2009). Table 1 shows the results. The B^3 metric is an extrinsic clustering evaluation metric and needs a gold standard set of clusters to evaluate against. The multiplicity B^3 works nicely for overlapping clusters: the metric does not need to match cluster IDs and only considers the number of the clusters that a pair of data points shares. For a pair of data points e and e', let $C(e)$ be the set of the test clusters that e belongs to, and $L(e)$ be the set of e's gold standard clusters. The multiplicity B^3 scores are evaluated as follows:

Airbus A320 family	**Super Bowl XLIII**
Air Force One	Arizona Cardinals
Chesley Sullenberger	Super Bowl
US Airways Flight 1549	Kurt Warner

2009 flu pandemic by country
Severe acute respiratory syndrome
2009 flu pandemic in the United States

Figure 6: Examples of clusters: K-means clustering on the articles of January 27, 2009 and May 12, 2009. The centroid article for each cluster, defined as the closest article to the center of the cluster in vector space, is in bold.

$$\text{Prec}(e, e') = \frac{\min\left(|C(e) \cap C(e')|, |L(e) \cap L(e')|\right)}{|C(e) \cap C(e')|}$$

$$\text{Recall}(e, e') = \frac{\min\left(|C(e) \cap C(e')|, |L(e) \cap L(e')|\right)}{|L(e) \cap L(e')|}$$

The overall B^3 scores are evaluated as follows:

$$\text{Prec} = \text{Avg}_e \text{Avg}_{e'.C(e) \cap C(e') \neq 0} \text{Prec}(e, e')$$

$$\text{Recall} = \text{Avg}_e \text{Avg}_{e'.L(e) \cap L(e') \neq 0} \text{Recall}(e, e')$$

The inter-annotator agreement in the B^3 scores are in the range of 67%–74%. K-means clustering performs best, achieving 79% precision compared to manual clustering. OneHop clustering using the link structure achieved comparable performance. LDA performed significantly worse, comparable to ConComp clustering.

Clustering the articles according to the relevance to recent popularity is not trivial even for humans. In WikiTopics articles for February 10, 2009, *Journey (band)* and *Bruce Springsteen* may seem to be relevant to *Grammy Awards*, but in fact they are relevant on this day because they performed the halftime show at the *Super Bowl*. K-means fails to recognize this and put them into the cluster of *Grammy Awards*, while ConComp merged *Grammy Awards* and *Super Bowl* into the same cluster. OneHop kept the two clusters intact and benefited from putting *Bruce Springsteen* into both the clusters. LDA clustering does not have such a benefit; its performance might have suffered from our allowing only a single membership for an article. Clustering using the link structure performs comparably with other clustering algorithms without using topic models. It is worth noting that there are a few "octopus" articles that have links to many articles. The *United States* on January 27, 2009 was disastrous, with its links to 58 articles, causing ConComp clustering to group 89 articles into a single cluster. OneHop clustering's condition that groups only articles that are one hop away alleviates the issue and it also benefited from putting an article into multiple clusters.

[6] K=50 worked reasonably well for the most cases. We are planning to explore a more principled way to set the number.

To see if external source help better clustering, we explored the use of news articles. We included the news articles that we crawled from various news websites into the same vector space as the Wikipedia articles, and ran K-means clustering with the same settings as before. For each day, we experimented with news articles within different numbers of past days. The results did not show significant improvement over clustering without external news articles. This needs further investigation[7].

4 Textualization

We would like to generate textual descriptions for the clustered articles to explain why they are popular and what current event they are relevant to. We started with a two-step approach similar to multi-document extractive summarization approaches (Mckeown et al., 2005). The first step is sentence selection; we extract the best sentence that describes the relevant event for each article. The second step is combining the selected sentences of a cluster into a coherent summary. Here, we focus on the first step of selecting a sentence and evaluate the selected sentences. The selected sentences for each cluster are then put together without modification, where the quality of generated summary mainly depends on the extracted sentences at the first step. We consider each article separately, using as features only information such as date expressions and references to the topic of the article. Future work will consider sentence extraction, aware of the related articles in the same cluster, and better summarization techniques, such as sentence fusion or paraphrasing.

We preprocess the Wikipedia articles using the Serif system (Boschee et al., 2005) for date tagging and coreference resolution. The identified temporal expressions are in various formats such as exact date ("February 12, 1809"), a season ("spring"), a month ("December 1808"), a date without a specific year ("November 19"), and even relative time ("now", "later that year", "The following year"). Some examples are shown in Figure 7. The entities mentioned in a given article are compiled into a list and the mentions of each entity, including pronouns, are linked to the entity as a coreference chain. Some examples are shown in Figure 9.

In our initial scheme, we picked the first sentence of each article because the first sentence is usually an overview of the topic of the article and often relevant to the current event. For example, a person's article often has the first line with one's recent achievement or death. An article about an album or a film often begins with the release date. We call this **First**.

[7]News articles tend to group with other news articles. We are currently experimenting with different filtering and parameters. Also note that we only experimented with all news articles on a given day. Clustering with selective news articles might help.

February 12, 1809	September
1860	Later that year
now	November 19
the 17th century	that same month
some time	The following winter
December 1808	The following year
34 years old	April 1865
spring	late 1863

Figure 7: Selected examples of temporal expressions identified by Serif from 247 such date and time expressions extracted from the article *Abraham Lincoln*.

We also picked the sentence with the most recent date to the day on which the article was selected. Dates in the near future are considered in the same way as the recent dates. Dates may appear in various formats, so we make a more specific format take precedence, i.e. "February 20, 2009" is selected over vaguer dates such as "February 2009" or "2009". We call this scheme **Recent**.

As the third scheme, we picked the sentence with the most recent date among those with a reference to the article's title. The reasoning behind this is if the sentence refers to the title of the article, it is more likely to be relevant to the current event. We call this scheme **Self**.

After selecting a sentence for each cluster, we substitute personal pronouns in the sentence with their proper names. This step enhances readability of the sentence, which often refers to people by a pronoun such as "he", "his", "she", or "her'. The examples of substituted proper names appear in Figure 9 in bold. The Serif system classifies which entity mentions are proper names for the same person, but choosing the best name among the names is not a trivial task: proper names may vary from *John* to *John Kennedy* to *John Fitzgerald "Jack" Kennedy*. We choose the most frequent proper name.

For fifty randomly chosen articles over the five selected days, two annotators selected the sentences that best describes why an article gained popularity recently, among 289 sentences per each article on average from the article text. For each article, annotators picked a single best sentence, and possibly multiple alternative sentences. If there is no such single sentence that best describes a relevant event, annotators marked none as the best sentence and listed alternative sentences that partially explain the relevant event. The evaluation results for all the selection schemes are shown in Table 2. To see inter-annotator agreement, two annotators' selections were evaluated against each other. The other selection schemes are evaluated against both the two annotators' selection and their scores in the table are averaged across the two. The precision and recall score for best sentences are determined by evaluating a scheme's selection of the

2009-01-27: *Inauguration of Barack Obama*

Gold: The inauguration of Barack Obama as the forty-fourth President of the United States took place on January 20, 2009.
Alternatives: 1. The inauguration, with a record attendance for any event held in Washington, D.C., marked the commencement of the four-year term of Barack Obama as President and Joseph Biden as Vice President. 2. With his inauguration as President of the United States, Obama became the first African American to hold the office and the first President born in Hawaii. 3. Official events were held in Washington, D.C. from January 18 to 21, 2009, including the We Are One: The Obama Inaugural Celebration at the Lincoln Memorial, a day of service on the federal observance of the Martin Luther King, Jr. Day, a "Kids' Inaugural: We Are the Future" concert event at the Verizon Center, the inaugural ceremony at the U.S. Capitol, an inaugural luncheon at National Statuary Hall, a parade along Pennsylvania Avenue, a series of inaugural balls at the Washington Convention Center and other locations, a private White House gala and an inaugural prayer service at the Washington National Cathedral.
First: The inauguration of Barack Obama as the forty-fourth President of the United States took place on January 20, 2009.
Recent: On January 22, 2009, a spokesperson for the Joint Committee on Inaugural Ceremonies also announced that holders of blue, purple and silver tickets who were unable to enter the Capitol grounds to view the inaugural ceremony would receive commemorative items.
Self: On January 21, 2009, President Obama, First Lady Michelle Obama, Vice President Biden and Dr. Jill Biden attended an inaugural prayer service at the Washington National Cathedral.

2009-02-10: *February 2009 Great Britain and Ireland snowfall*

Gold: The snowfall across Great Britain and Ireland in February 2009 is a prolonged period of snowfall that began on 1 February 2009.
Alternative: Many areas experienced their largest snowfall levels in 18 years.
First: The snowfall across Great Britain and Ireland in February 2009 is a prolonged period of snowfall that began on 1 February 2009.
Recent: BBC regional summary - 4 February 2009
Self: The snowfall across Great Britain and Ireland in February 2009 is a prolonged period of snowfall that began on 1 February 2009.

2009-04-19: *Wilkins Sound*

Gold: On 5 April 2009 the thin bridge of ice to the Wilkins Ice Shelf off the coast of Antarctica splintered, and scientists expect it could cause the collapse of the Shelf.
Alternatives: 1. There are reports the shelf has exploded into hundreds of small ice bergs. 2. On 5 April 2009, the ice bridge connecting part of the ice shelf to Charcot Island collapsed.
First: Wilkins Sound is a seaway in Antarctica that is largely occupied by the Wilkins Ice Shelf.
Recent: On 5 April 2009 the thin bridge of ice to the Wilkins Ice Shelf off the coast of Antarctica splintered, and scientists expect it could cause the collapse of the Shelf.
Self: On 25 March 2008 a chunk of the Wilkins ice shelf disintegrated, putting an even larger portion of the glacial ice shelf at risk.

Figure 8: Sentence selection: **First** selects the first sentence, and often fails to relate the current event. **Recent** tend to pinpoint the exact sentence that describes the relevant current event, but fails when there are several sentences with a recent temporal expression. **Self** helps avoid sentences that does not refer to the topic of the article, but suffers from errors propagated from coreference resolution.

2009-01-27: *Barack Obama*
Before: He was inaugurated as President on January 20, 2009.
After: *Obama* was inaugurated as President on January 20, 2009.
Coref: {Barack Hussein Obama II (brk hsen obm; born August 4,, Barack Obama, Barack Obama as the forty-fourth President, Barack Obama, Sr. , Crain's Chicago Business naming Obama, Michelle Obama, Obama, Obama in Indonesian, Senator Obama,}

2009-02-10: *Rebirth (Lil Wayne album)*
Before: He also stated the album will be released on April 7, 2009.
After: *Lil Wayne* also stated the album will be released on April 7, 2009.
Coref: {American rapper Lil Wayne, Lil Wayne, Wayne}

2009-04-19: *Phil Spector*
Before: His second trial resulted in a conviction of second degree murder on April 13, 2009.
After: *Spector's* second trial resulted in a conviction of second degree murder on April 13, 2009.
Coref: {Mr. Spector, Phil Spector, Phil Spector" The character of Ronnie "Z, Spector, Spector-, Spector (as a producer), Spector himself, Spector of second-degree murder, Spector, who was conducting the band for all the acts,, Spektor, wife Ronnie Spector}

2009-05-12: *Eminem*
Before: He is planning on releasing his first album since 2004, Relapse, on May 15, 2009.
After: *Eminem* is planning on releasing his first album since 2004, Relapse, on May 15, 2009.
Coref: {Eminem, Marshall Bruce Mathers, Marshall Bruce Mathers III, Marshall Bruce Mathers III (born October 17,, Mathers}

2009-10-12: *Brett Favre*
Before: He came out of retirement for the second time and signed with the Minnesota Vikings on August 18, 2009.
After: *Favre* came out of retirement for the second time and signed with the Minnesota Vikings on August 18, 2009.
Coref: {Bonita Favre, Brett Favre, Brett Lorenzo Favre, Brett's father Irvin Favre, Deanna Favre, Favre, Favre,, Favre (ISBN 978-1590710364) which discusses their personal family and Green Bay Packers family, Irvin Favre, Southern Miss. Favre, the Brett Favre, The following season Favre, the jersey Favre}

Figure 9: Pronoun replacement: Personal pronouns are substituted with their proper names, which are *italicized*. The coreference chain for the entity is also shown; our method correctly avoids names wrongly placed in the chain. Note that unlike the other sentences, the last one is not related to the current event, Brett Favre's victory against Green Bay Packers.

Scheme	Single best		Alternatives	
	Precision	Recall	Precision	Recall
Human	0.50	0.55	0.85	0.75
First	0.14	0.20	0.33	0.40
Recent	0.31	0.44	0.51	0.60
Self	0.31	0.36	0.49	0.48
Self fallback	**0.33**	**0.46**	**0.52**	**0.62**

Table 2: Textualization: evaluation results of sentence selection schemes. Self fallback scheme first tries to select the best sentence as the Self scheme, and if it fails to select one it falls back to the Recent scheme.

best sentences against a gold standard's selection. To evaluate alternative sentences, precision is measured as the fraction of articles where the test and gold standard selections overlap (share at least one sentence), compared to the total number of articles that have at least one sentence selected according to the test set. Recall is defined by instead dividing by the number of articles that have at least one sentence selected in the gold standard.

The low inter-annotator agreement for selecting the best sentence shows the difficulty of the task. However, when their sentence selection is evaluated by allowing multiple alternative gold standard sentences, the agreement is higher. It seems that there are a set of articles for which it is easy to pick the best sentence that two annotators and automatic selection schemes easily agree on, and another set of articles for which it is difficult to find such a sentence. In the *easier* articles, the best sentence often includes a recent date expression, which is easily picked up by the Recent scheme. Figure 8 illustrates such cases. In the more difficult articles, there are no such sentences with recent dates. *X2 (film)* is such an example; it was released in 2003. The release of the prequel *X-Men Origins: Wolverine* in 2009 renewed its popularity and the *X2 (film)* article still does not have any recent dates. There is a more subtle case: the article *Farrah Fawcett* includes many sentences with recent dates in a section, which describes the development of a recent event. It is hard to pinpoint the best one among them.

Sentence selection heavily depends on other NLP components, so errors in them could result in the error in sentence selection. *Serena Williams* is an example where an error in sentence splitting propagates to sentence selection. The best sentence manually selected was the first sentence in the article "Serena Jameka Williams . . . , as of February 2, 2009, is ranked World No. 1 by the Women's Tennis Association . . . ." The sentence was disastrously divided into two sentences right after "No." by NLTK during preprocessing. In other words, the gold standard sentence could not be selected no matter how well selection performs. Another source of error propagation is coreference resolution. The Self scheme limits sentence selection to the sentences with a reference to the articles' title, and it failed to improve over Recent. In qualitative analysis, 3 out of 4 cases that made a worse choice resulted from failing to recognize a reference to the topic of the article. By having it fall back to Recent's selection when it failed to find any best sentence, its performance marginally improved. Improvements of the components would result in better performance of sentence selection.

WikiTopics's current sentence extraction succeeded in generating the best or alternative sentences that summarizes the relevant current event for more than half of the articles, in enhanced readability through coreference resolution. For the other difficult cases, it needs to take different strategies rather than looking for the most recent date expressions. Alternatives may consider references to other related articles. In future work, selected sentences will be combined to create summary of a current event, and will use sentence compression, fusion and paraphrasing to create more succinct summaries.

5 Related work

WikiTopics's pipeline architecture resembles that of news summarization systems such as Columbia Newsblaster (McKeown et al., 2002). Newsblaster's pipeline is comprised of components for performing web crawls, article text extraction, clustering, classification, summarization, and web page generation. The system processes a constant stream of newswire documents. In contrast, WikiTopics analyzes a static set of articles. Hierarchical clustering like three-level clustering of Newsblaster (Hatzivassiloglou et al., 2000) could be applied to WikiTopics to organize current events hierarchically. Summarizing multiple sentences that are extracted from the articles in the same cluster would provide a comprehensive description about the current event. Integer linear programming-based models (Woodsend and Lapata, 2010) may prove to be useful to generate summaries while global constraints like length, grammar, and coverage are met.

The problem of Topic Detection and Tracking (TDT) is to identify and follow new events in newswire, and to detect the first story about a new event (Allan et al., 1998). Allan et al. (2000) evaluated a variety of vector space clustering schemes, where the best settings from those experiments were then used in our work. This was followed recently by Petrović et al. (2010), who took an approximate approach to first story detection, as applied to Twitter in an on-line streaming setting. Such a system might provide additional information to WikiTopics by helping to identify and describe current events that have yet to be explicitly described in a Wikipedia article. Svore et al. (2007) explored enhancing single-document summariation using news query logs, which may also be applicable to WikiTopics.

Wikipedia's inter-article links have been utilized to

construct a topic ontology (Syed et al., 2008), word segmentation corpora (Gabay et al., 2008), or to compute semantic relatedness (Milne and Witten, 2008). In our work, we found the link structure to be as useful to cluster topically related articles as well as the article text. In future work, the text and the link structure will be combined as Chaudhuri et al. (2009) explored multi-view hierarchical clustering for Wikipedia articles.

6 Conclusions

We have described a pipeline for article selection, clustering, and textualization in order to identify and describe significant current events as according to Wikipedia content, and metadata. Similarly to Wikipedia editors maintaining that site's "current events" pages, we are concerned with neatly collecting articles of daily relevance, only automatically, and more in line with expressed user interest (through the use of regularly updated page view logs). We have suggested that Wikipedia's hand-curated articles cannot be predicted solely based on pageviews. Clustering methods based on topic models and inter-article link structure are shown to be useful to group a set of articles that are coherently related to a current event. Clustering based on only link structure achieved comparable performance with clustering based on topic models. In a third of cases, the sentence that best described a current event could be extracted from the article text based on temporal expressions within an article. We employed a coreference resolution system assist in text generation, for improved readability. As future work, sentence compression, fusion, and paraphrasing could be applied to selected sentences with various strategies to more succinctly summarize the current events. Our approach is language independent, and may be applied to multi-lingual current event detection, exploiting further the online encyclopedia's cross-language references. Finally, we plan to leverage social media such as Twitter as an additional signal, especially in cases where essential descriptive information has yet to be added to a Wikipedia article of interest.

Acknowledgments

We appreciate Domas Mituzas and Frédéric Schütz for the pageviews statistics and Peter Skomoroch for the Trending Topics software. We also thank three anonymous reviewers for their thoughtful advice. This research was supported in part by the NSF under grant IIS-0713448 and the EC through the EuroMatrixPlus project. The first author was funded by Samsung Scholarship. Opinions, interpretations, and conclusions are those of the authors and not necessarily endorsed by the sponsors.

References

James Allan, Jaime Carbonell, George Doddington, Jonathan Yamron, and Yiming Yang. 1998. Topic Detection and Tracking Pilot Study Final Report. In *Proceedings of the DARPA Broadcast News Transcription and Understanding Workshop*.

James Allan, Victor Lavrenko, Daniella Malin, and Russell Swan. 2000. Detections, bounds, and timelines: UMass and TDT-3. In *Proceedings of Topic Detection and Tracking Workshop*.

Enrique Amigó, Julio Gonzalo, Javier Artiles, and Felisa Verdejo. 2009. A comparison of extrinsic clustering evaluation metrics based on formal constraints. *Inf. Retr.*, 12(4):461–486.

D.M. Blei, A.Y. Ng, and M.I. Jordan. 2003. Latent Dirichlet allocation. *Journal of Machine Learning Research*.

Elizabeth Boschee, Ralph Weischedel, and Alex Zamanian. 2005. Automatic information extraction. In *Proceedings of IA*.

Kamalika Chaudhuri, Sham M. Kakade, Karen Livescu, and Karthik Sridharan. 2009. Multi-view clustering via canonical correlation analysis. In *Proceedings of ICML*.

David Gabay, Ziv Ben-Eliahu, and Michael Elhadad. 2008. Using wikipedia links to construct word segmentation corpora. In *Proceedings of AAAI Workshops*.

Vasileios Hatzivassiloglou, Luis Gravano, and Ankineedu Maganti. 2000. An investigation of linguistic features and clustering algorithms for topical document clustering. In *Proceedings of SIGIR*.

Edward Loper and Steven Bird. 2002. NLTK: the Natural Language Toolkit. In *Proceedings of ACL*.

C. Manning, P. Raghavan, and H. Schütze. 2008. *Introduction to information retrieval*. Cambridge University Press.

Andrew Kachites McCallum. 2002. MALLET: A Machine Learning for Language Toolkit. http://mallet.cs.umass.edu.

Kathleen R. McKeown, Regina Barzilay, David Evans, Vasileios Hatzivassiloglou, Judith L. Klavans, Ani Nenkova, Carl Sable, Barry Schiffman, and Sergey Sigelman. 2002. Tracking and summarizing news on a daily basis with Columbia's Newsblaster. In *Proceedings of HLT*.

Kathleen Mckeown, Rebecca J. Passonneau, David K. Elson, Ani Nenkova, and Julia Hirschberg. 2005. Do summaries help? a task-based evaluation of multi-document summarization. In *Proceedings of SIGIR*.

David Milne and Ian H. Witten. 2008. An effective, low-cost measure of semantic relatedness obtained from Wikipedia links. In *Proceedings of AAAI Workshops*.

Saša Petrović, Miles Osborne, and Victor Lavrenko. 2010. Streaming first story dectection with application to Twitter. In *Proceedings of NAACL*.

Krysta M. Svore, Lucy Vanderwende, and Christopher J.C. Burges. 2007. Enhancing single-document summarization by combining ranknet and third-party sources. In *Proceedings of EMNLP-CoLing*.

Zareen Saba Syed, Tim Finin, and Anupam Joshi. 2008. Wikipedia as an ontology for describing documents. In *Proceedings of ICWSM*.

Kristian Woodsend and Mirella Lapata. 2010. Automatic generation of story highlights. In *Proceedings of ACL*.

Abstractive Summarization of Line Graphs from Popular Media

Charles F. Greenbacker **Peng Wu**
Sandra Carberry **Kathleen F. McCoy** **Stephanie Elzer***
Department of Computer and Information Sciences
University of Delaware, Newark, Delaware, USA
[charlieg|pwu|carberry|mccoy]@cis.udel.edu
*Department of Computer Science
Millersville University, Millersville, Pennsylvania, USA
elzer@cs.millersville.edu

Abstract

Information graphics (bar charts, line graphs, etc.) in popular media generally have a discourse goal that contributes to achieving the communicative intent of a multimodal document. This paper presents our work on abstractive summarization of line graphs. Our methodology involves hypothesizing the intended message of a line graph and using it as the core of a summary of the graphic. This core is then augmented with salient propositions that elaborate on the intended message.

1 Introduction

Summarization research has focused primarily on summarizing textual documents, and until recently, other kinds of communicative vehicles have been largely ignored. As noted by Clark (1996), language is more than just words — it is any signal that is intended to convey a message. Information graphics (non-pictorial graphics such as bar charts, line graphs, etc.) in popular media such as *Newsweek*, *Businessweek*, or newspapers, generally have a communicative goal or intended message. For example, the graphic in Figure 1 is intended to convey a changing trend in sea levels — relatively flat from 1900 to 1930 and then rising from 1930 to 2003. Thus, using Clark's view of language, information graphics are a means of communication.

Research has shown that the content of information graphics in popular media is usually not repeated in the text of the accompanying article (Carberry et al., 2006). The captions of such graphics are also often uninformative or convey little of the graphic's high-level message (Elzer et al., 2005). This contrasts with scientific documents in which graphics are often used to visualize data, with explicit references to the graphic being used to explain their content (e.g., "*As shown in Fig. A...*"). Information graphics in popular media contribute to the overall communicative goal of a multimodal document and should not be ignored.

Our work is concerned with the summarization of information graphics from popular media. Such summaries have several major applications: 1) they can be integrated with the summary of a multimodal document's text, thereby producing a richer summary of the overall document's content; 2) they can be stored in a digital library along with the graphic itself and used to retrieve appropriate graphics in response to user queries; and 3) for individuals with sight impairments, they can be used along with a screen reader to convey not only the text of a document, but also the content of the document's graphics. In this paper we present our work on summarizing line graphs. This builds on our previous efforts into summarizing bar charts (Demir et al., 2008; Elzer et al., 2011); however, line graphs have different messages and communicative signals than bar charts and their continuous nature requires different processing. In addition, a very different set of visual features must be taken into account in deciding the importance of including a proposition in a summary.

2 Methodology

Most summarization research has focused on extractive techniques by which segments of text are extracted and put together to form the summary.

Proceedings of the Workshop on Automatic Summarization for Different Genres, Media, and Languages, pages 41–48,
Portland, Oregon, June 23, 2011. ©2011 Association for Computational Linguistics

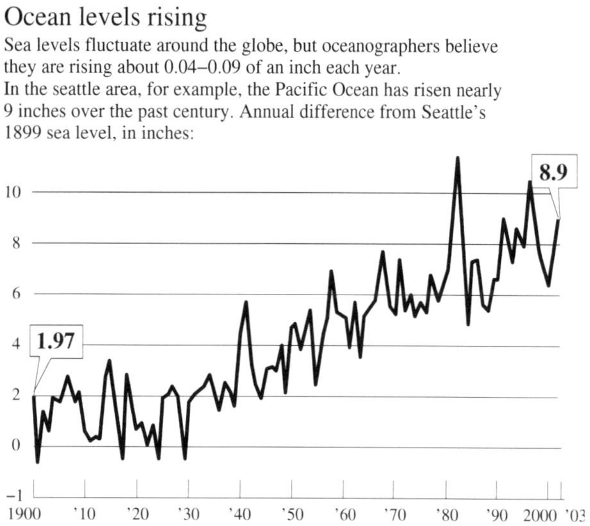

Figure 1: From "Worry flows from Arctic ice to tropical waters" in USA Today, May 31, 2006.

However, the *Holy Grail* of summarization work is abstractive summarization in which the document's content is understood and the important concepts are integrated into a coherent summary. For information graphics, extractive summarization might mean treating the text in the graphic (e.g., the caption) as if it were document text. One could imagine perhaps expanding this view to include selecting particular data points or segments and constructing sentences that convey them. Abstractive summarization, on the other hand, requires that the high-level content of the graphic be identified and conveyed in the summary. The goal of our work is abstractive summarization. The main issues are identifying the knowledge conveyed by a graphic, selecting the concepts that should be conveyed in a summary, and integrating them into coherent natural language sentences.

As noted in the Introduction, information graphics in popular media generally have a high-level message that they are intended to convey. This message constitutes the primary communicative or discourse goal (Grosz and Sidner, 1986) of the graphic and captures its main contribution to the overall discourse goal of the entire document. However, the graphic also includes salient features that are important components of the graphic's content. For example, the graphic in Figure 1 is very jagged with sharp fluctuations, indicating that short-term changes have been inconsistent. Since the graphic's intended message represents its primary discourse goal, we contend that this message should form the core or focus of the graphic's summary. The salient features should be used to augment the summary of the graph and elaborate on its intended message. Thus, our methodology consists of the following steps: 1) hypothesize the graphic's primary discourse or communicative goal (i.e., its intended message), 2) identify additional propositions that are salient in the graphic, and 3) construct a natural language summary that integrates the intended message and the additional salient propositions into a coherent text.

Section 3 presents our methodology for hypothesizing a line graph's intended message or discourse goal. It starts with an XML representation of the graphic that specifies the x-y coordinates of the sampled pixels along the data series in the line graph, the axes with tick marks and labels, the caption, etc.; constructing the XML representation is the responsibility of a Visual Extraction Module similar to the one for bar charts described by Chester and Elzer (2005). Section 4 presents our work on identifying the additional propositions that elaborate on the intended message and should be included in the summary. Section 5 discusses future work on realizing the propositions in a natural language summary, and Section 6 reviews related work in multimodal and abstractive summarization.

3 Identifying a Line Graph's Message

Research has shown that human subjects have a strong tendency to use line graphs to portray trend relationships, as well as a strong tendency to describe line graphs in terms of trends (Zacks and Tversky, 1999). We analyzed a corpus of simple line graphs collected from various popular media including *USA Today*, *Businessweek*, and *The (Wilmington) News Journal*, and identified a set of 10 high-level message categories that capture the kinds of messages that are conveyed by a simple line graph. Table 1 defines four of them. The complete list can be found in (Wu et al., 2010b). Each of these messages requires recognizing the visual trend(s) in the depicted data. We use a support vector machine (SVM) to first segment the line graph into a sequence of visually-distinguishable trends; this sequence is then input into a Bayesian network that reasons with evidence from the graphic

Intention Category	Description
RT: Rising-trend	There is a rising trend from <param$_1$> to <param$_2$>.
CT: Change-trend	There is a <direction$_2$> trend from <param$_2$> to <param$_3$> that is significantly different from the <direction$_1$> trend from <param$_1$> to <param$_2$>.
CTR: Change-trend-return	There is a <direction$_1$> trend from <param$_3$> to <param$_4$> that is different from the <direction$_2$> trend between <param$_2$> and <param$_3$> and reflects a return to the kind of <direction$_1$> trend from <param$_1$> to <param$_2$>.
BJ: Big-jump	There was a very significant sudden jump in value between <param$_1$> and <param$_2$> which may or may not be sustained.

Table 1: Four categories of High Level Messages for Line Graphs

in order to recognize the graphic's intended message. The next two subsections outline these steps. (Our corpus of line graphs can be found at www.cis.udel.edu/~carberry/Graphs/viewallgraphs.php)

3.1 Segmenting a Line Graph

A line graph can consist of many short, jagged line segments, although a viewer of the graphic abstracts from it a sequence of visually-distinguishable trends. For example, the line graph in Figure 1 consists of two trends: a relatively stable trend from 1900 to 1930 and a longer, increasing trend from 1930 to 2003. Our Graph Segmentation Module (GSM) takes a top-down approach (Keogh et al., 2001) to generalize the line graph into sequences of rising, falling, and stable segments, where a segment is a series of connected data points. The GSM starts with the entire line graph as a single segment and uses a learned model to recursively decide whether each segment should be split into two subsegments; if the decision is to split, the division is made at the point being the greatest distance from a straight line between the two end points of the original segment. This process is repeated on each subsegment until no further splits are identified. The GSM returns a sequence of straight lines representing a linear regression of the points in each subsegment, where each straight line is presumed to capture a visually-distinguishable trend in the original graphic.

We used Sequential Minimal Optimization (Platt, 1999) in training an SVM to make segment splitting decisions. We chose to use an SVM because it works well with high-dimensional data and a relatively small training set, and lessens the chance of overfitting by using the maximum margin separating hyperplane which minimizes the worst-case generalization errors (Tan et al., 2005). 18 attributes, falling into two categories, were used in building the data model (Wu et al., 2010a). The first category captures statistical tests computed from the sampled data points in the XML representation of the graphic; these tests estimate how different the segment is from a linear regression (i.e., a straight line). The second category of attributes captures global features of the graphic. For example, one such attribute relates the segment size to the size of the entire graphic, based on the hypothesis that segments comprising more of the total graph may be stronger candidates for splitting than segments that comprise only a small portion of the graph.

Our Graph Segmentation Module was trained on a set of 649 instances that required a split/no-split decision. Using leave-one-out cross validation, in which one instance is used for testing and the other 648 instances are used for training, our model achieved an overall accuracy rate of 88.29%.

3.2 A Bayesian Recognition System

Once the line graph has been converted into a sequence of visually-distinguishable trends, a Bayesian network is built that captures the possible intended messages for the graphic and the evidence for or against each message. We adopted a Bayesian network because it weighs different pieces of evidence and assigns a probability to each candidate intended message. The next subsections briefly outline the Bayesian network and its evaluation; details can be found in (Wu et al., 2010b).

Structure of the Bayesian Network Figure 2 shows a portion of the Bayesian network constructed for Figure 1. The top-level node in our Bayesian network represents all of the high-level message cat-

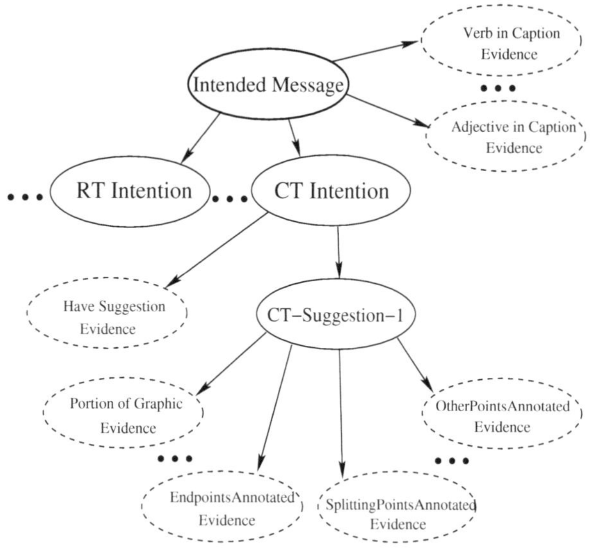

Figure 2: A portion of the Bayesian network

egories. Each of these possible non-parameterized message categories is repeated as a child of the top-level node; this is purely for ease of representation. Up to this point, the Bayesian network is a static structure with conditional probability tables capturing the a priori probability of each category of intended message. When given a line graph to analyze, an extension of this network is built dynamically according to the particulars of the graph itself. Candidate (concrete) intended messages, having actual instantiated parameters, appear beneath the high-level message category nodes. These candidates are introduced by a Suggestion Generation Module; it dynamically constructs all possible intended messages with concrete parameters using the visually-distinguishable trends (rising, falling, or stable) identified by the Graph Segmentation Module. For example, for each visually-distinguishable trend, a Rising, Falling, or Stable trend message is suggested; similary, for each sequence of two visually-distinguishable trends, a Change-trend message is suggested. For the graphic in Figure 1, six candidate messages will be generated, including RT(1930, 2003), CT(1900, stable, 1930, rise, 2003) and BJ(1930, 2003) (see Table 1).

Entering Evidence into the Bayesian Network Just as listeners use evidence to identify the intended meaning of a speaker's utterance, so also must a viewer use evidence to recognize a graphic's intended message. The evidence for or against each of the candidate intended messages must be entered into the Bayesian network. We identified three kinds of evidence that are used in line graphs: attention-getting devices explicitly added by the graphic designer (e.g., the annotation of a point with its value), aspects of a graphic that are perceptually-salient (e.g., the slope of a segment), and clues that suggest the general message category (e.g., a verb [or noun derived from a verb such as *rebound*] in the caption which might indicate a Change-trend message). The first two kinds of evidence are attached to the Bayesian network as children of each candidate message node, such as the child nodes of "CT-Suggestion-1" in Figure 2. The third kind of evidence is attached to the top level node as child nodes named "Verb in Caption Evidence" and "Adjective in Caption Evidence" in Figure 2.

Bayesian Network Inference We evaluated the performance of our system for recognizing a line graph's intended message on a corpus of 215 line graphs using leave-one-out cross validation in which one graph is held out as a test graph and the conditional probability tables for the Bayesian network are computed from the other 214 graphs. Our system recognized the correct intended message with the correct parameters for 157 line graphs, resulting in a 73.36% overall accuracy rate.

4 Identifying Elaborative Propositions

Once the intended message has been determined, the next step is to identify additional important informational propositions[1] conveyed by the line graph which should be included in the summary. To accomplish this, we collected data to determine what kinds of propositions in what situations were deemed most important by human subjects, and developed rules designed to make similar assessments based on the graphic's intended message and visual features present in the graphic.

4.1 Collecting Data from Human Subjects

Participants in our study were given 23 different line graphs. With each graph, the subjects were provided

[1]We define a "proposition" as a logical representation describing a relationship between one or more concepts, while a "sentence" is a surface form realizing one or more propositions.

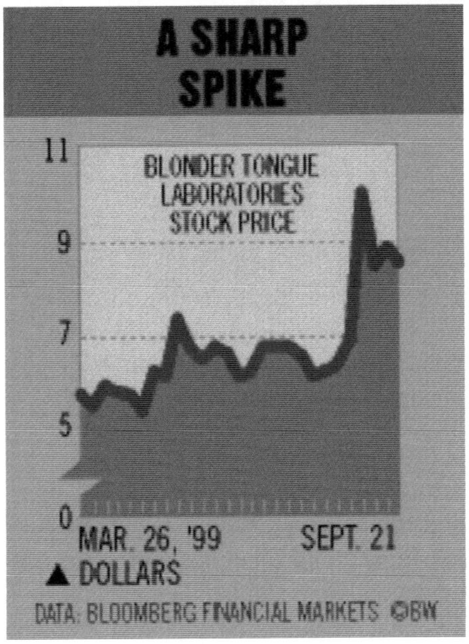

Figure 3: From "This Cable Outfit Is Getting Tuned In" in *Businessweek* magazine, Oct 4, 1999.

with an initial sentence describing the overall intended message of the graphic. The subjects were asked to add additional sentences so that the completed summary captured the most important information conveyed by the graphic. The graphs were presented to the subjects in different orders, and the subjects completed as many graphs as they wanted during the one hour study session. The set covered the eight most prevalent of our intended message categories and a variety of visual features. Roughly half of the graphs were real-world examples from the corpus used to train the Bayesian network in Section 3.2, (e.g., Figure 3), with the others created specifically to fill a gap in the coverage of intended messages and visual features.

We collected a total of 998 summaries written by 69 human subjects for the 23 different line graphs. The number of summaries we received per graph ranged from 37 to 50. Most of the summaries were between one and four sentences long, in addition to the initial sentence (capturing the graphic's intended message) that was provided for each graph. A representative sample summary collected for the line graph shown in Figure 3 is as follows, with the initial sentence provided to the study participants in italics:

> *This line graph shows a big jump in Blonder Tongue Laboratories stock price in August '99.* The graph has many peaks and valleys between March 26th 1999 to August '99 but maintains an average stock price of around 6 dollars. However, in August '99 the stock price jumps sharply to around 10 dollars before dropping quickly to around 9 dollars by September 21st.

4.2 Extracting & Weighting Propositions

The data collected during the study was analyzed by a human annotator who manually coded the propositions that appeared in each individual summary in order to determine, for each graphic, which propositions were used and how often. For example, the set of propositions coded in the sample summary from Section 4.1 were:

- $volatile(26Mar99, Aug99)$
- $average\_val(26Mar99, Aug99, \$6)$
- $jump\_1(Aug99, \$10)$
- $steep(jump\_1)$
- $decrease\_1(Aug99, \$10, 21Sep99, \$9)$
- $steep(decrease\_1)$

From this information, we formulated a set of rules governing the use of each proposition according to the intended message category and various visual features. Our intuition was that by finding and exploiting a correlation between the intended message category and/or certain visual features and the propositions appearing most often in the human-written summaries, our system could use these indicators to determine which propositions are most salient in new graphs. Our rules assign a weight to each proposition in the situation captured by the rule; these weights are based on the relative frequency of the proposition being used in summaries reflecting similar situations in our corpus study. The rules are organized into three types:

1. Message Category-only (M):
   IF $M = m$ **THEN** select P with weight w_1
2. Visual Feature-only (V):
   IF $V = v$ **THEN** select P with weight w_2
3. Message Category + Visual Feature:
   IF $M = m$ and $V = v$
   THEN select P with weight w_2

We constructed type 1 (Message Category-only) rules when a plurality of human-written summaries in our corpus for all line graphs belonging to a given message category contain the proposition. A weight was assigned according to the frequency with which the proposition was included. This weighting, shown in Equation 1, is based on the proportion of summaries for each line graph in the corpus having intended message *m* and containing proposition *P*.

$$w_1 = \prod_{i=1}^{n} \frac{P_i}{S_i} \tag{1}$$

In this equation, n is the number of line graphs in this intended message category, S_i is the total number of summaries for a particular line graph with this intended message category, and P_i is the number of these summaries that contain the proposition.

Intuitively, a proposition appearing in all summaries for all graphs in a given message category will have a weight of 1.0, while a proposition which never appears will have a weight of zero. However, a proposition appearing in all summaries for half of the graphs in a category, and rarely for the other half of the graphs in that category, will have a much lower weight than one which appears in half of the summaries for all the graphs in that category, even though the overall frequencies could be equal for both. In this case, the message category is an insufficient signal, and it is likely that the former proposition is more highly correlated to some particular visual feature than to the message category.

Weights for type 2 and type 3 rules (Visual Feature-only and Message Category + Visual Feature) are slightly more complicated in that they involve a measure of degree for the associated visual feature rather than simply its presence. The definition of this measure varies depending on the nature of the visual feature (e.g., steepness of a trend line, volatility), but all such measures range from zero to one. Additionally, since the impact of a visual feature is a matter of degree, the weighting cannot rely on a simple proportion of summaries containing the proposition as in type 1 rules. Instead, it is necessary to find the covariance between the magnitude of the visual feature ($|v|$) and how frequently the corresponding proposition is used ($\frac{P}{S}$) in the corpus summaries for the n graphs having this visual feature, as shown in Equation 2.

$$Cov(|v|, \frac{P}{S}) = \left[\left(\frac{\sum_{i=1}^{n}|v_i|}{n}\frac{\sum_{i=1}^{n}\frac{P_i}{S_i}}{n}\right) - \frac{\sum_{i=1}^{n}|v_i|\frac{P_i}{S_i}}{n}\right] \tag{2}$$

Then for a particular graphic whose magnitude for this feature is $|\overline{v}|$, we compute the weight w_2 for the proposition P as shown in Equation 3.

$$w_2 = |\overline{v}| * Cov(|v|, \frac{P}{S}) \tag{3}$$

This way, the stronger a certain visual feature is in a given line graph, the higher the weight for the associated proposition.

Type 3 rules (Message Category + Visual Feature) differ only from type 2 rules in that they are restricted to a particular intended message category, rather than any line graph having the visual feature in question. For example, a proposition comparing the slope of two trends may be appropriate for a graph in the Change-trend message category, but does not make sense for a line graph with only a single trend (e.g., Rising-trend).

Once all propositions have been extracted and ranked, these weights are passed along to a graph-based content selection framework (Demir et al., 2010) that iteratively selects for inclusion in the initial summary those propositions which provide the best coverage of the highest-ranked information.

4.3 Sample Rule Application

Figures 1 and 4 consist of two different line graphs with the same intended message category: Change-trend. Figure 1 shows a stable trend in annual sea level difference from 1900 to 1930, followed by a rising trend through 2003, while Figure 4 shows a rising trend in Durango sales from 1997 to 1999, followed by a falling trend through 2006. Propositions associated with type 1 rules will have the same weights for both graphs, but propositions related to visual features may have different weights. For example, the graph in Figure 1 is far more volatile than the graph in Figure 4. Thus, the type 2 rule associated with volatility will have a very high weight for the graph in Figure 1 and will almost certainly be included in the initial summary of that line graph (e.g.,

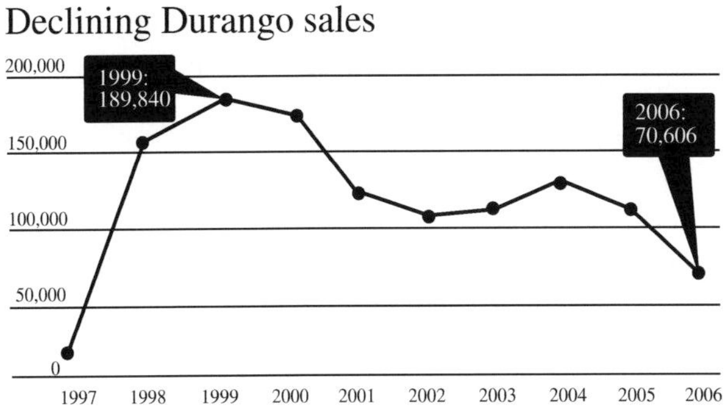

Figure 4: From "Chrysler: Plant had $800 million impact" in The (Wilmington) News Journal, Feb 15, 2007.

"*The values vary a lot...*", "*The trend is unstable...*"), possibly displacing a type 1 proposition that would still appear in the summary for the graph in Figure 4.

5 Future Work

Once the propositions that should be included in the summary have been selected, they must be coherently organized and realized as natural language sentences. We anticipate using the FUF/SURGE surface realizer (Elhadad and Robin, 1996); our collected corpus of line graph summaries provides a large set of real-world expressions to draw from when crafting the surface realization forms our system will produce for the final-output summaries. Our summarization methodology must also be evaluated. In particular, we must evaluate the rules for identifying the additional informational propositions that are used to elaborate the overall intended message, and the quality of the summaries both in terms of content and coherence.

6 Related Work

Image summarization has focused on constructing a smaller image that contains the important content of a larger image (Shi et al., 2009), selecting a set of representative images that summarize a collection of images (Baratis et al., 2008), or constructing a new diagram that summarizes one or more diagrams (Futrelle, 1999). However, all of these efforts produce an image as the end product, not a textual summary of the content of the image(s).

Ferres et al. (2007) developed a system for conveying graphs to blind users, but it generates the same basic information for each instance of a graph type (e.g., line graphs) regardless of the individual graph's specific characteristics. Efforts toward summarizing multimodal documents containing graphics have included naïve approaches relying on captions and direct references to the image in the text (Bhatia et al., 2009), while content-based image analysis and NLP techniques are being combined for multimodal document indexing and retrieval in the medical domain (Névéol et al., 2009).

Jing and McKeown (1999) approached abstractive summarization as a text-to-text generation task, modifying sentences from the original document via editing and rewriting. There have been some attempts to do abstractive summarization from semantic models, but most of it has focused on text documents (Rau et al., 1989; Reimer and Hahn, 1988), though Alexandersson (2003) used abstraction and semantic modeling for speech-to-speech translation and multilingual summary generation.

7 Discussion

Information graphics play an important communicative role in popular media and cannot be ignored. We have presented our methodology for constructing a summary of a line graph. Our method is abstractive, in that we identify the important high-level knowledge conveyed by a graphic and capture it in propositions to be realized in novel, coherent natural language sentences. The resulting summary can be integrated with a summary of the document's text to produce a rich summary of the entire multimodal document. In addition, the graphic's summary can be used along with a screen reader to provide sight-impaired users with full access to the knowledge conveyed by multimodal documents.

Acknowledgments

This work was supported in part by the National Institute on Disability and Rehabilitation Research under Grant No. H133G080047.

References

Jan Alexandersson. 2003. *Hybrid Discourse Modeling and Summarization for a Speech-to-Speech Translation System*. Ph.D. thesis, Saarland University.

Evdoxios Baratis, Euripides Petrakis, and Evangelos Milios. 2008. Automatic web site summarization by image content: A case study with logo and trademark images. *IEEE Transactions on Knowledge and Data Engineering*, 20(9):1195–1204.

Sumit Bhatia, Shibamouli Lahiri, and Prasenjit Mitra. 2009. Generating synopses for document-element search. In *Proceeding of the 18th ACM Conference on Information and Knowledge Management*, CIKM '09, pages 2003–2006, Hong Kong, November. ACM.

Sandra Carberry, Stephanie Elzer, and Seniz Demir. 2006. Information graphics: an untapped resource for digital libraries. In *Proc. of the 29th Annual Int'l ACM SIGIR Conf. on Research & Development in Information Retrieval*, SIGIR '06, pages 581–588, Seattle, August. ACM.

Daniel Chester and Stephanie Elzer. 2005. Getting computers to see information graphics so users do not have to. In *Proceedings of the 15th International Symposium on Methodologies for Intelligent Systems (LNAI 3488)*, ISMIS 2005, pages 660–668, Saratoga Springs, NY, June. Springer-Verlag.

Herbert Clark. 1996. *Using Language*. Cambridge University Press.

Seniz Demir, Sandra Carberry, and Kathleen F. McCoy. 2008. Generating textual summaries of bar charts. In *Proceedings of the 5th International Natural Language Generation Conference*, INLG 2008, pages 7–15, Salt Fork, Ohio, June. ACL.

Seniz Demir, Sandra Carberry, and Kathleen F. McCoy. 2010. A discourse-aware graph-based content-selection framework. In *Proceedings of the 6th International Natural Language Generation Conference*, INLG 2010, pages 17–26, Trim, Ireland, July. ACL.

Michael Elhadad and Jacques Robin. 1996. An overview of SURGE: a re-usable comprehensive syntactic realization component. In *Proceedings of the 8th International Natural Language Generation Workshop (Posters & Demos)*, Sussex, UK, June. ACL.

Stephanie Elzer, Sandra Carberry, Daniel Chester, Seniz Demir, Nancy Green, Ingrid Zukerman, and Keith Trnka. 2005. Exploring and exploiting the limited utility of captions in recognizing intention in information graphics. In *Proceedings of the 43rd Annual Meeting of the Association for Computational Linguistics*, pages 223–230, Ann Arbor, June. ACL.

Stephanie Elzer, Sandra Carberry, and Ingrid Zukerman. 2011. The automated understanding of simple bar charts. *Artificial Intelligence*, 175:526–555, February.

Leo Ferres, Petro Verkhogliad, Gitte Lindgaard, Louis Boucher, Antoine Chretien, and Martin Lachance. 2007. Improving accessibility to statistical graphs: the iGraph-Lite system. In *Proc. of the 9th Int'l ACM SIGACCESS Conf. on Computers & Accessibility*, ASSETS '07, pages 67–74, Tempe, October. ACM.

Robert P. Futrelle. 1999. Summarization of diagrams in documents. In I. Mani and M. Maybury, editors, *Advances in Automatic Text Summarization*. MIT Press.

Barbara Grosz and Candace Sidner. 1986. Attention, Intentions, and the Structure of Discourse. *Computational Linguistics*, 12(3):175–204.

Hongyan Jing and Kathleen R. McKeown. 1999. The decomposition of human-written summary sentences. In *Proc. of the 22nd Annual Int'l ACM SIGIR Conf. on Research & Development in Information Retrieval*, SIGIR '99, pages 129–136, Berkeley, August. ACM.

Eamonn J. Keogh, Selina Chu, David Hart, and Michael J. Pazzani. 2001. An online algorithm for segmenting time series. In *Proceedings of the 2001 IEEE International Conference on Data Mining*, ICDM '01, pages 289–296, Washington, DC. IEEE.

Aurélie Névéol, Thomas M. Deserno, Stéfan J. Darmoni, Mark Oliver Güld, and Alan R. Aronson. 2009. Natural language processing versus content-based image analysis for medical document retrieval. *Journal of the American Society for Information Science and Technology*, 60(1):123–134.

John C. Platt. 1999. Fast training of support vector machines using sequential minimal optimization. In B. Schölkopf, C. J. C. Burges, and A. J. Smola, editors, *Advances in kernel methods: support vector learning*, pages 185–208. MIT Press, Cambridge, MA, USA.

Lisa F. Rau, Paul S. Jacobs, and Uri Zernik. 1989. Information extraction and text summarization using linguistic knowledge acquisition. *Information Processing & Management*, 25(4):419 – 428.

Ulrich Reimer and Udo Hahn. 1988. Text condensation as knowledge base abstraction. In *Proceedings of the 4th Conference on Artificial Intelligence Applications*, CAIA '88, pages 338–344, San Diego, March. IEEE.

Liang Shi, Jinqiao Wang, Lei Xu, Hanqing Lu, and Changsheng Xu. 2009. Context saliency based image summarization. In *Proceedings of the 2009 IEEE international conference on Multimedia and Expo*, ICME '09, pages 270–273, New York. IEEE.

Pang-Ning Tan, Michael Steinbach, and Vipin Kumar. 2005. *Introduction to Data Mining*. Addison Wesley.

Peng Wu, Sandra Carberry, and Stephanie Elzer. 2010a. Segmenting line graphs into trends. In *Proceedings of the 2010 International Conference on Artificial Intelligence*, ICAI '10, pages 697–703, Las Vegas, July.

Peng Wu, Sandra Carberry, Stephanie Elzer, and Daniel Chester. 2010b. Recognizing the intended message of line graphs. In *Proc. of the 6th Int'l Conf. on Diagrammatic Representation & Inference*, Diagrams '10, pages 220–234, Portland. Springer-Verlag.

Jeff Zacks and Barbara Tversky. 1999. Bars and lines: A study of graphic communication. *Memory & Cognition*, 27:1073–1079.

Extractive Multi-Document Summaries Should Explicitly Not Contain Document-Specific Content

Rebecca Mason and Eugene Charniak
Brown Laboratory for Linguistic Information Processing (BLLIP)
Brown University
Providence, RI 02912
{rebecca,ec}@cs.brown.edu

Abstract

Unsupervised approaches to multi-document summarization consist of two steps: finding a content model of the documents to be summarized, and then generating a summary that best represents the most salient information of the documents. In this paper, we present a sentence selection objective for extractive summarization in which sentences are penalized for containing content that is specific to the documents they were extracted from. We modify an existing system, HIERSUM (Haghighi & Vanderwende, 2009), to use our objective, which significantly outperforms the original HIERSUM in pairwise user evaluation. Additionally, our ROUGE scores advance the current state-of-the-art for both supervised and unsupervised systems with statistical significance.

1 Introduction

Multi-document summarization is the task of generating a single summary from a set of documents that are related to a single topic. Summaries should contain information that is relevant to the main ideas of the entire document set, and should not contain information that is too specific to any one document. For example, a summary of multiple news articles about the *Star Wars* movies could contain the words "Lucas "and "Jedi", but should not contain the name of a fan who was interviewed in one article. Most approaches to this problem generate summaries *extractively*, selecting whole or partial sentences from the original text, then attempting to piece them together in a coherent manner. Extracted text is selected based on its relevance to the main ideas of the document set. Summaries can be evaluated manually, or with automatic metrics such as ROUGE (Lin, 2004).

The use of structured probabilistic topic models has made it possible to represent document set content with increasing complexity (Daumé & Marcu, 2006; Tang et al., 2009; Celikyilmaz & Hakkani-Tur, 2010). Haghighi and Vanderwende (2009) demonstrated that these models can improve the quality of generic multi-document summaries over simpler surface models. Their most complex hierarchial model improves summary content by teasing out the words that are not general enough to represent the document set as a whole. Once those words are no longer included in the content word distribution, they are *implicitly* less likely to appear in the extracted summary as well. But this objective does not sufficiently keep document-specific content from appearing in multi-document summaries.

In this paper, we present a selection objective that *explicitly* excludes document-specific content. We re-implement the HIERSUM system from Haghighi and Vanderwende (2009), and show that using our objective dramatically improves the content of extracted summaries.

2 Modeling Content

The easiest way to model document content is to find a probability distribution of all unigrams that appear in the original documents. The highest frequency words (after removing stop words) have a high likelihood of appearing in human-authored summaries (Nenkova & Vanderwende, 2005). However, the raw

Proceedings of the Workshop on Automatic Summarization for Different Genres, Media, and Languages, pages 49–54,
Portland, Oregon, June 23, 2011.

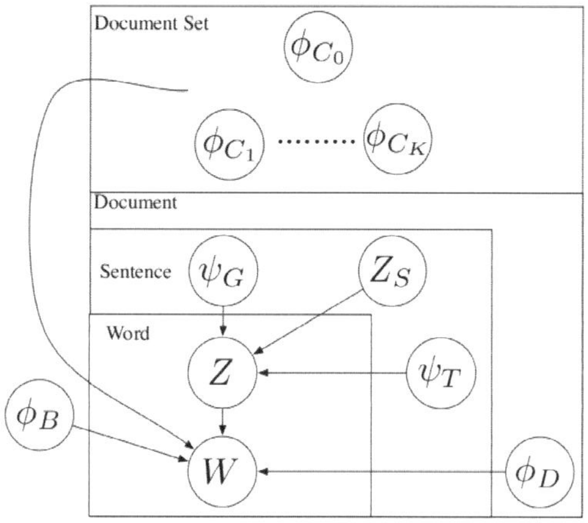

Figure 1: The graphical model for HIERSUM (Haghighi & Vanderwende, 2009).

unigram distribution may contain words that appear frequently in one document, but do not reflect the content of the document set as a whole.

Probabilistic topic models provide a more principled approach to finding a distribution of content words. This idea was first presented by Daumé and Marcu (2006) for their BAYESUM system for query-focused summarization, and later adapted for non-query summarization in the TOPICSUM system by Haghighi and Vanderwende (2009). [1] In these systems, each word from the original documents is drawn from one of three vocabulary distributions. The first, ϕ_b, is the background distribution of general English words. The second, ϕ_d, contains vocabulary that is specific to that one document. And the third, ϕ_c, is the distribution of content words for that document set, and contains relevant words that should appear in the generated summary.

HIERSUM (Haghighi & Vanderwende, 2009) adds more structure to TOPICSUM by further splitting the content distribution into multiple sub-topics. The content words in each sentence can be generated by either the general content topic or the content sub-topic for that sentence, and the words from the general content distribution are considered when building the summary.

[1]The original BAYESUM can also be used without a query, in which case, BAYESUM and TOPICSUM are the exact same model.

3 KL Selection

The KL-divergence between two unigram word distributions P and Q is given by $KL(P||Q) = \sum_w P(w) \log \frac{P(w)}{Q(w)}$. This quantity is used for summary sentence selection in several systems including Lerman and McDonald (2009) and Haghighi and Vanderwende (2009), and was used as a feature in the discrimitive sentence ranking of Daumé and Marcu (2006).

TOPICSUM and HIERSUM use the following KL objective, which finds $\mathbf{S}*$, the summary that minimizes the KL-divergence between the estimated content distribution ϕ_c and the summary word distribution $P_{\mathbf{S}}$:

$$\mathbf{S}* = \min_{\mathbf{S}:|\mathbf{S}|\leq L} KL(\phi_c||P_{\mathbf{S}})$$

A greedy approximation is used to find $\mathbf{S}*$. Starting with an empty summary, sentences are greedily added to the summary one at a time until the summary has reached the maximum word limit, L. The values of $P_{\mathbf{S}}$ are smoothed uniformly in order to ensure finite values of $KL(\phi_c||P_{\mathbf{S}})$.

4 Why Document-Specific Words are a Problem

The KL selection objective effectively ensures the presence of highly weighted content words in the generated summary. But it is asymmetric in that it allows a high proportion of words in the summary to be words that appear infrequently, or not at all, in the content word distribution. This asymmetry is the reason why the KL selection metric does not sufficiently keep document-specific words out of the generated summary.

Consider what happens when a document-specific word is included in summary $\mathbf{S}$. Assume that the word w_i does not appear (has zero probability) in the content word distribution ϕ_c, but does appear in the document-specific distribution ϕ_d for document d. Then w_i appearing in $\mathbf{S}$ has very little impact on $KL(\phi_c||P_{\mathbf{S}}) = \sum_j \phi_c(w_j) \log \frac{\phi_c(w_j)}{P_{\mathbf{S}}(w_j)}$ because $\phi_c(w_i) = 0$. There will be a slight impact because the presence of the word w_i in $\mathbf{S}$ will cause the probability of other words in the summary to be sligntly smaller. But in a summary of length 250 words (the length used for the DUC summarization task) the difference is negligible.

The reason why we do not simply substitute a symmetrical metric for comparing distributions (e.g., Information Radius) is because we want the selection objective to disprefer *only* document-specific words. Specifically, the selection objective should not disprefer background English vocabulary.

5 KL(c)-KL(d) Selection

In contrast to the KL selection objective, our objective measures the similarity of both content and document-specific word distributions to the extracted summary sentences. We combine these measures linearly:

$$\mathbf{S}* = \min_{\mathbf{S}:|\mathbf{S}|\leq L} KL(\phi_c||P_{\mathbf{S}}) - KL(\phi_d||P_{\mathbf{S}})$$

Our objective can be understood in comparison to the MMR criterion by (Carbonell & Goldstein, 1998), which also utilizes a linear metric in order to maximize informativeness of summaries while minimizing some unwanted quality of the extracted sentences (in their case, redundancy). In contrast, our criterion utilizes information about what kind of information should *not* be included in the summary, which to our knowledge has not been done in previous summarization systems.[2]

For comparison to the previous KL objective, we also use a greedy approximation for $\mathbf{S}*$. However, because we are extracting sentences from many documents, the distribution ϕ_d is actually several distributions, a separate distribution for each document in the document set. The implementation we used in our experiments is that, as we consider a sentence s to be added to the previously selected sentences $\mathbf{S}$, we set ϕ_d to be the document-specific distribution of the document that s has been extracted from. So each time we add a sentence to the summary, we find the sentence that minimizes $KL(\phi_c||P_{\mathbf{S}\cup s}) - KL(\phi_{d(s)}||P_{\mathbf{S}\cup s})$. Another implementation we tried was combining all of the ϕ_d distributions into one distribution, but we did not notice any difference in the extracted summaries.

[2]A few anonymous reviewers asked if we tried to optimize the value of λ for $KL(\phi_c||P_{\mathbf{S}}) - \lambda KL(\phi_d||P_{\mathbf{S}})$. The answer is yes, but optimizing λ to maximize ROUGE results in summaries that are perceptibly worse, and manually tuning λ did not seem to produce any benefit.

6 Evaluation

6.1 Data

We developed our sentence selection objective using data from the Document Understanding Conference[3] (DUC) 2006 summarization task, and used data from DUC 2007 task for evaluations. In these tasks, the system is given a set of 25 news articles related to an event or topic, and needs to generate a summary of under 250 words from those documents.[4] For each document set, four human-authored summaries are provided for use with evaluations. The DUC 2006 data has 50 document sets, and the DUC 2007 data has 45 document sets.

6.2 Automatic Evaluation

Systems are automatically evalatued using ROUGE (Lin, 2004), which has good correlation with human judgments of summary content. ROUGE compares n-gram recall between system-generated summaries, and human-authored reference summaries. The first two metrics we compare are unigram and bigram recall, R-1 and R-2, respectively. The last metric, R-SU4, measures recall of skip-4 bigrams, which may skip one or two words in between the two words to be measured. We set ROUGE to stem both the system and reference summaries, scale our results by 10^2 and present scores with and without stopwords removed.

The ROUGE scores of the original HIERSUM system are given in the first row of table 1, followed by the scores of HIERSUM using our KL(c-d) selection. The KL(c-d) selection outperforms the KL selection in each of the ROUGE metrics shown. In fact, these results are statistically significant over the baseline KL selection for all but the unigram metrics (R-1 with and without stopwords). These results show that our KL(c-d) selection yields significant improvements in terms of ROUGE performance, since having fewer irrelevant words in the summaries leaves room for words that are more relevant to the content topic, and therefore more likely to appear in the reference summaries.

The last two rows of table 1 show the scores of two recent state-of-the-art multi-document sum-

[3]http://duc.nist.gov/

[4]Some DUC summarization tasks also provide a query or focus for the summary, but we ignore these in this work.

System	ROUGE w/o stopwords			ROUGE w/ stopwords		
	R-1	R-2	R-SU4	R-1	R-2	R-SU4
HIERSUM w/ KL	34.6	7.3	10.4	43.1	9.7	15.3
HIERSUM w/ KL(c)-KL(d)	35.6	**9.9**	**12.8**	43.2	**11.6**	**16.6**
PYTHY	35.7	8.9	12.1	42.6	11.9	16.8
HYBHSUM	35.1	8.3	11.8	45.6	11.4	17.2

Table 1: ROUGE scores on the DUC 2007 document sets. The first two rows compare the results of the unigram HIERSUM system with its original and our improved selection metrics. Bolded scores represent where our system has a significant improvement over the orignal HIERSUM. For further comparison, the last two rows show the ROUGE scores of two other state-of-the-art multi-document summarization systems (Toutanova et al., 2007; Celikyilmaz & Hakkani-Tur, 2010). See section 6.2 for more details.

marization systems. Both of these systems select sentences discriminatively on many features in order to maximize ROUGE scores. The first, PYTHY (Toutanova et al., 2007), trains on dozens of sentence-level features, such as n-gram and skip-gram frequency, named entities, sentence length and position, and also utilizes sentence compression. The second, HYBHSUM (Celikyilmaz & Hakkani-Tur, 2010), uses a nested Chinese restaurant process (Blei et al., 2004) to model a hierarchical content distribution with more complexity than HIERSUM, and uses a regression model to predict scores for new sentences.

For both of these systems, our summaries are significantly better for R-2 and R-SU4 without stopwords, and comparable in all other metrics.[5] These results show that our selection objective can make a simple unsupervised model competitive with more complicated supervised models.

6.3 Manual Evaluation

For manual evaluation, we performed a pairwise comparison of summaries generated by HIERSUM with both the original and our modified sentence selection objective. Users were given the two summaries to compare, plus a human-generated reference summary. The order that the summaries appeared in was random. We asked users to select which summary was better for the following questions:[6]

System	Q1	Q2	Q3	Q4
HIERSUM w/ KL	29	36	31	36
. . . w/ KL(c)-KL(d)	58	51	56	51

Table 2: Results of manual evaluation. Our criterion outperforms the original HIERSUM for all attributes, and is significantly better for Q1 and Q3. See section 6.3 for details.

Q1 Which was better in terms of overall content?

Q2 Which summary had less repetition?

Q3 Which summary was more coherent?

Q4 Which summary had better focus?

We took 87 pairwise preferences from participants over Mechanical Turk.[7] The results of our evaluation are shown in table 2. For all attributes, our criterion performs better than the original HIERSUM selection criterion, and our results for Q1 and Q3 are significantly better as determined by Fisher sign test (two-tailed P value < 0.01).

These results confirm that our objective noticably improves the content of extractive summaries by selecting sentences that contain less document-specific

[5] Haghighi and Vanderwende (2009) presented a version of HIERSUM that models documents as a bag of bigrams, and provides results comparable to PYTHY. However, the bigram HIERSUM model does not find consistent bags of bigrams.

[6] These are based on the manual evaluation questions from DUC 2007, and are the same questions asked in Haghighi and Vanderwende (2009).

[7] In order to ensure quality results, we asked participants to write a sentence on why they selected their preference for each question. We also monitored the time taken to complete each comparison. Overall, we rejected about 25% of responses we received, which is similar to the percentage of responses rejected by Gillick and Liu (2010).

information. This leaves more room in the summary for content that is relevant to the main idea of the document set (Q1) and keeps out content that is not relevant (Q4). Additionally, although neither criterion explicitly addresses coherence, we found that a significant proportion of users found our summaries to be more coherent (Q3). We believe this may be the case because the presence of document-specific information can distract from the main ideas of the summary, and make it less likely that the extracted sentences will flow together.

There is no immediate explanation for why users found our our summaries less repetitive (Q2), since if anything the narrowing of topics due to the negative $KL(\phi_d||P_S)$ term should make for more repetition. We currently hypothesize that the improved score is simply a spillover from the general improvement in document quality.

7 Conclusion

We have described a new objective for sentence selection in extractive multi-document summarization, which is different in that it explicitly gives negative weight to sentences that contain document-specific words. Our objective significantly improves the performance of an existing summarization system, and improves on current best ROUGE scores with significance.

We have observed that while the content in our extracted summaries is often comparable to the content in human-written summaries, the extracted summaries are still far weaker in terms of coherence and repetition. Even though our objective significantly improves coherence, more sophisticated methods of decoding are still needed to produce readable summaries. These problems could be addressed through further refinement of the selection objective, through simplification or compression of selected sentences, and through improving the coherence of generated summaries.

References

Blei, D. M., Griffiths, T. L., Jordan, M. I., & Tenenbaum, J. B. (2004). Hierarchical topic models and the nested chinese restaurant process. *Advances in Neural Information Processing Systems*.

Carbonell, J., & Goldstein, J. (1998). The use of mmr, diversity-based reranking for reordering documents and producing summaries. *Proceedings of the 21st annual international ACM SIGIR conference on Research and development in information retrieval* (pp. 335–336). New York, NY, USA: ACM.

Celikyilmaz, A., & Hakkani-Tur, D. (2010). A hybrid hierarchical model for multi-document summarization. *Proceedings of the 48th Annual Meeting of the Association for Computational Linguistics* (pp. 815–824). Stroudsburg, PA, USA: Association for Computational Linguistics.

Daumé, III, H., & Marcu, D. (2006). Bayesian query-focused summarization. *ACL-44: Proceedings of the 21st International Conference on Computational Linguistics and the 44th annual meeting of the Association for Computational Linguistics* (pp. 305–312). Morristown, NJ, USA: Association for Computational Linguistics.

Gillick, D., & Liu, Y. (2010). Non-expert evaluation of summarization systems is risky. *Proceedings of the NAACL HLT 2010 Workshop on Creating Speech and Language Data with Amazon's Mechanical Turk* (pp. 148–151). Stroudsburg, PA, USA: Association for Computational Linguistics.

Haghighi, A., & Vanderwende, L. (2009). Exploring content models for multi-document summarization. *Proceedings of Human Language Technologies: The 2009 Annual Conference of the North American Chapter of the Association for Computational Linguistics* (pp. 362–370). Boulder, Colorado: Association for Computational Linguistics.

Lerman, K., & McDonald, R. (2009). Contrastive summarization: an experiment with consumer reviews. *Proceedings of Human Language Technologies: The 2009 Annual Conference of the North American Chapter of the Association for Computational Linguistics, Companion Volume: Short Papers* (pp. 113–116). Stroudsburg, PA, USA: Association for Computational Linguistics.

Lin, C.-Y. (2004). Rouge: a package for automatic evaluation of summaries. *Proceedings of the Workshop on Text Summarization Branches Out (WAS 2004)*. Barcelona, Spain.

Nenkova, A., & Vanderwende, L. (2005). *The impact of frequency on summarization* (Technical Report). Microsoft Research.

Tang, J., Yao, L., & Chen, D. (2009). Multi-topic based query-oriented summarization. *SDM'09* (pp. 1147–1158).

Toutanova, K., Brockett, C., Gamon, M., Jagarlamudi, J., Suzuki, H., & Vanderwende, L. (2007). The PYTHY Summarization System: Microsoft Research at DUC 2007. *Proc. of DUC*.

Author Index